THE SOCIOPATH CLUB

THE JACKAL

Dedication

For those who love the hunt just as I do.

Acknowledgment

To all sociopaths, narcissists, psychopaths and serial
killers. We are always family.

Table Of Contents

INTRODUCTION

What is a Jackal? They are a species of carnivores. They are cooperative, cunning hunters and the most active at dawn and dusk. They defend their territory from others by chasing away intruders and marking their territory as a warning sign to all.

The Jackal has a bad reputation. Some believe they are friends of the night whose howls are the haunting songs of their prey. Others dismiss them as coldhearted, calculated killers. A trickster.

The Jackal can adapt to its circumstances— dodging unnecessary danger and avoiding other predators or hunters. They are intelligent and loyal creatures that live a social, cooperative existence.

A life living on the edge comes at a price, however. Be careful of who you surround yourself with and what you become because the Jackal is fearless and will always be there for you to succumb to its own desires.

These are general facts; however, I am more than this definition. But before I tell you my story, I want you to read Owen's and his beginning.

CHAPTER 1

Owen Riley slowly opened his eyes to the beeping of his alarm clock. "Turn it off dude," his roommate yelled at him from across the room. "It's been going off for 30 seconds already."

"Sorry," Owen said half awake. He reached out and turned it off as he turned to his back and stretched. "College is fun they said," he thought to himself. New freedoms. No parents. No responsibilities. Very little money. He chuckled. He rolled out of bed and sifted through some of his clothes -smelling which one of his shirts could pass another day.

Within minutes he was ready. He grabbed his book bag and checked the time. No time for breakfast. It wasn't as if he could afford it anyway. He had money in his account to cover food every quarter, but he preferred the buffet which costs more, so you cut out here and there to make it work.

"See ya Cliff," Owen yelled at his roommate and out the door he went.

Cliff waved while he continued the finishing touches on a paper due that morning. A bagel hung out of his mouth.

Owen went to the bathroom that was shared with a floor of about 20 other guys in the dorm. He looked over to the stall while he urinated to see high heels and obviously a woman sitting on the toilet.

"Nice shoes. Is that you Jones?" he laughed.

"Whaaaat?" a hung-over woman's voice returned. He shook his head and laughed as he zipped up and washed his hands.

He headed out the door when another student yelled at him. "Bookbag." Owen turned and yelled thanks and left toward his class. He walked through the yard and checked the time. He had enough time to walk through the cafeteria. Everyone's classes started at different times and maybe he could score some leftover anything on someone's tray. He was in luck.

"You going to finish that dude?" Owen asked another student who looked down at his leftover in disgust.

"No, knock yourself out man," he said.

Owen didn't care. You get what you can when you can and however you could to survive. He was in college. He received a scholarship, but it only covered for the basics like your room, books, and food. For anything else, he would have to work and earn it or ask his parents. They wouldn't give him anything. They were not happy that he was even here. His parents owned a small-town grocery store and were hoping that Owen would take it over.

The key word was a small town. No one wants to stay in a small town at eighteen. They want to go out and adventure. See the world. Experience everything. The big city. A place you could get lost in and mess up and nobody knows who you are. Where you go to a rock concert with a thousand other people and get lost in the crowd. Not in a small town where everyone knew when you got a ticket, or a band would stop through just to get gas and leave.

He grew up in the Midwest. The closest city was about 40 minutes away. Not bad but still too far. There was no mall, no museum, no nothing. They had a rundown bowling alley, and they had a movie house that showed the same movie for a month at a time. Two restaurants and two fast food places but that was it. Owen wanted more.

"You have everything you need right here," His father would say. "What else do you want?"

"What if something happens to us and we have to see a Doctor?" Owen would say in return.

"There's a doctor's office up the street. A clinic in town. If it's something bigger, we go to the city less than an hour away," his dad would say in return.

"Owen honey," mom would calm them both. "Why don't you just go to the city for the summer and work there and see what it's like? Trust me; you'll miss home and come back."

"Good idea Mary," Dad would say. "That's why all the city folk come out here. Fishing and hunting."

Owen did go to the city that summer. He also visited the colleges and sent out all the paperwork hoping that somewhere near an ocean would offer him a scholarship. They didn't, but one college four hours from his house did and there he was on that campus instead. He reassured his parents that he was only four hours away and could come back if they needed anything.

It still didn't settle well with them. But this was his life, not theirs. He didn't want to stay in some small town on the border of Canada and stock shelves and order supplies and carry groceries to someone's car every day. He wanted more out of life. Besides, he had four younger siblings. They could do it.

His parents made it clear that this was his choice and they weren't happy about it, and he was on his own. No money from them. He understood and shrugged his shoulders as he left. Mom slipped him $200 she had been saving and all that was pretty much gone in the first two weeks he came.

Owen was bound and determined to make this work. He wanted to be a psychiatrist and a writer. A strange combo to his father. He even tried to explain that he wanted to help people with their problems and then, in his spare time, write. "You can write here," Dad yelled and pointed to an area in the yard. "I'll build you an area. Look at that view."

Owen appreciated the offer, but he had to try. If he tried and failed, he would return. But he had to try. He had to know if this was what he wanted to do for life. By the end of the first quarter, he knew he picked the right field. A psychiatrist from a facility called Medical Lake came by and talked all afternoon about their facility and the patients he had helped. He even showed a film featuring some of his patients.

After class, Owen knew he was in the right field. He would document all of his patients throughout his career. He would make lots of money and be able to travel to exotic places meanwhile curing patients and living in a huge house with his future wife and children. His parents would tell him he was right about everything and they were wrong. He would end his career by publishing a book of his lifetime achievements and probably winning awards for the book and opening the door for others who would follow in his footpath.

Owen smiled at his fantasy as another student walked by, saying he was late for class. "Here, I'll dump that for you," Owen offered. The student thought nothing of it and handed Owen a tray full of leftover biscuits and gravy. "Rich kids are so wasteful," Owen smiled and ate.

A few girls walked by and saw what Owen was doing and rolled their eyes and laughed and walked away. He didn't care. He had hot food in his stomach and was ready for the day. "Shit," he said out loud as he saw the clock. Dr. Forsythe's class started in 11 minutes and if he was not in the class at the top of the hour, the door would not be opened for him or for anyone for any reason -no matter how rich you were. Dr. Forsythe locked the door immediately.

Owen grabbed onto his book bag and booked it across campus. After almost knocking down three other students, he got into class and sat down just as Dr. Forsythe was heading up to the door. He wasn't the only student running in either. Several other girls and boys ran into the class as Dr. Forsythe closed the door. A few unlucky ones were shut out. You could hear the profanity from the other students in the hallway as he locked the door and immediately started the lesson of the day.

"It doesn't matter if you're God. The class begins at 0900 sharp. If you're late, you lose out. Many of you pampered privileged people," he began looking over at the elite who sat together and grinned at the rest of the class, "do not know what true responsibility is. Anyway, let us begin….."

The lecture began. Owen took notes for the entire 50 minutes and for that entire time, Dr. Forsythe spoke. He hardly looked at notes. He was about in his mid-50's and he had experience. He had been a psychiatric Doctor for 25 years and now taught the next generation all he knew and what to expect. He gave great examples of patients he had over his career and how he helped them and how they helped him.

His experience and knowledge were superior. He had several quarks about himself too. Not only was he strict about time but he also had a nervous tick. He blinked a lot, and he would sometimes suddenly turn to see if someone was behind him. Like he heard noises that no one else heard. He would stop suddenly when speaking and take a deep breath on certain topics as if he was reliving the moment. It gave the stories an intensity and surreal feeling.

Owen could tell he wasn't impressed with the elite. Most of them were there to fulfill a class requirement but Owen wasn't. He craved this knowledge and experience.

"Tomorrow, I will be handing back your first paper you did, and I can't tell you how disappointed I was in some of you and surprised by others," he said, looking around.

Owen waited for their eyes to meet to see which category he fell into, but the class held about 75 students and all he was doing was glancing over everyone. There were three papers due and then the big one at the end of the year. Those three papers equaled about 25% of your grade and the final was another 50%. The tests were only worth 25%. It was a different way of grading than most teachers graded but it was his class and his rules.

Dr. Forsythe gave no extra credit. No retakes. His tests were multiple choice so if you took good notes, you were golden. The papers were the key. They came with rules also. They all had to be typed, double spaced and on certain quality of paper. They had to be at least 10 pages long, with the final paper 50 pages long. He gave the topic of all papers. The first one Owen had received a C on it. This was the second one. The next one would be announced tomorrow along with the final topic.

Owen had two weeks to do the next one and to the end of the entire quarter to finish the last one.

He took a deep breath. Class ended and everyone started getting up.

Everyone's schedule was different. Owen had an hour break before his next class. He had two classes back-to-back and then had another hour break and one more class and his day was done. Not a bad schedule for the first quarter. Next quarter would be more intense.

He put his books away and got up and looked over at Dawson Myer's paper. He had doodled the entire class. He never took one note. Owen shook his head and left. "What's his problem?" Carson responded when he saw Owen's reaction. They all looked over at him and Owen just continued.

In between classes, Owen spent time in the library. It was quiet and he could catch up on reading and doing work. He also could look through books of all the different places he would travel to when he graduated. He smiled.

Owen usually sat in the same spot. Second level is by the window and near the bathroom. He glanced out the window. Snow still covered parts of the ground. Spring couldn't get here fast enough for him. He heard a bunch of loud students coming up the stairway.

It was Dawson and his friends. They headed to another section of the library. Dawson was an elite. Rich parents. Dawson was there on a football scholarship. He drove a Mustang and had nice clothes and all the girls in school followed him. He hung around the same group of friends he had since High School. Every now and then, a new person would try to enter their posse, they would never let them in.

Dawson was a nice guy, but Owen just didn't like him. There was no reason. Perhaps it was the typical "You have but I don't" attitude. Dawson always nodded at him when he saw Owen.

Owen looked away and back at his homework due for the next three classes. He had more important stuff to worry about.

Later in the evening, after dinner, Owen and Cliff headed to the common room area. They were showing a movie. Some of the guys invited ladies from other fraternities and some, like him, were just alone. He watched the movie and enjoyed the treats the dorm provided and went back upstairs to play some videogames before going to bed.

He was eager to see what grade he would get on his paper. His other three classes were B average so all he had to do was pull a C or better to pass this quarter. He still had one more paper and then the mini-thesis. Next semester would be more psychology classes and English classes. This quarter and next, he was finishing up the rest of the math and other prerequisites he needed.

Owen set his alarm and his phone alarm for backup. He could hear his neighbor having sex. He sighed and put the pillow over his head and went to sleep.

CHAPTER 2
THROAT PUNCH

Owen watched Dr. Forsythe pass back everyone's test results. With so many students, it took about 20 minutes just to pass out results and then 20 minutes to go over the top missed topics or explanations of what everyone did wrong as a whole. Then he would drop the bombshell of what the next topic was before dismissing the class. Everything else would be detailed on the computer on his webpage he had set up for the class. Most of his communication was done through email.

He got to Owen's section and started handing out papers. He handed one to the girl who sat behind Owen and said, "One more grade like this,

Miss Fuller and you're out of the program." She looked surprised and disappointed. She took the sheet and sat down, embarrassed.

Most of Dr. Forsythe's comments were the same. "One more and you're out of the program." "I expected more detail from you." "Nice job. You're on your way." He stopped in front of Owen and Owen smiled. "I expected more detail, Mr. Riley. One more grade like this and you're out of the program." Owen's heart sank as he took the paper.

He heard the snickers from the elite. He glanced at the "D" on his page and looked over at Dawson. Dawson didn't make eye contact but Carson, Sawyer, Lincoln and Aldridge did. All of them held up their "As" for him to see. He read the comments on his well-written paper.

Dr. Forsythe felt it was lacking and missing key points. His direction was there but then wandered off-target in one area. He sank in his seat. He turned the paper over and waited to hear what the next topic would be so he wouldn't miss out. He felt depressed. He felt like all eyes were on him. He looked around the room and everyone seemed to be feeling the same. Everyone looked like they got throat punched.

"Your next paper is why do you want to be a psychiatrist and how do you plan to show the world and your colleagues you picked the right career," he began. Owen chuckled. This didn't sound like a college paper. This sounded like a grade school; what did you do on your summer vacation paper.

Sawyer raised his hand and Dr. Forsythe pointed at him. "What if I'm not becoming a psychiatrist? I'm just here for the credits, man?" Everyone laughed.

"Then pretend man," Dr. Forsythe responded. Everyone clapped and laughed.

"Now your final paper counts as 50% of your final grade and which many of you will need…. actually, all of you will need to have a C or greater to pass the course. For many of you, this will determine if you keep your scholarships," he began. Everyone sat up straighter and brought out paper and a pen. He continued. "I know that all of you, because I checked," he started, "also have English this quarter so this paper will also count as your English final." Everyone gasped.

"This was great," Owen thought. "Knock out two papers at once." Why was everyone freaking?

"That's not fair," One girl yelled and slammed her pen on the counter.

"I think it's awesome," another agreed with Owen's thought. "Get two done for one."

"What if my English teacher gives me an A and you give me a C?" one kid yelled across the room.

"ENOUGH," Dr. Forsythe yelled and slammed a book on the desk. It got quiet. "Life isn't fair. This is college. You will not argue with me. Your English grade will be based on your grammar and sentence structure which you have been practicing for 12 years. You have spell check so use it. Make sure to check for punctuation. She will grade you on that. I will grade you only on topic and content of subject material. I will give you that all today before you leave."

Everyone sat up, including the elite. He continued. "I know I'm hard on you. I get that. Some of you don't know this or have heard rumors that one of your classmates committed suicide last week." Everyone looked around. Dr. Forsythe held up his hand. "Not in our class but in the Engineering Department. A student failed his classes. Two of them were kicked out of the program. His parents were disappointed and he took his life. He jumped off a building in the city."

Gasps could be heard. Sawyer looked away. Owen watched as kids looked at the floor or fought back tears. No one probably knew this student but the fact that it was so easy and so complete to die at such a young age hit home.

Dr. Forsythe sighed and stood up and walked to the front of the room and leaned against desk. "I'm going to tell you something I've never told any of my other classes or students." Owen leaned forward. Dawson sat up and put his finger up as his girlfriend was trying to tell him something. She looked toward the teacher.

Dr. Forsythe began. "The young man who committed suicide was my son." The class gasped and went quiet again. "I put a lot of pressure on him and all of you to succeed. This paper on why you want to be a psychiatrist is a project on which all of you will get an A on if you type it, double-space it and hand it in on time. Each paper is expected to be 5 pages long. Make sure there are no spelling errors or it's a drop in your letter grade. This paper is a gift for you. This will save many of you so you don't lose your scholarships. It will bring people up to a C or better average.

The final paper is the big one. The instructions will be posted on the web page. Your topic is listed by your name on the door when you leave today. I now dismiss you. I will see you all next quarter and by then, many of you should have an outline on what your paper will look like. We will spend the first couple days of class, in sections, going over and approving or disproving your outline. If you are approved, you will move on to your paper. I will be here daily to help you with your papers otherwise the entire quarter, you're on your own to work on your paper. Now class dismissed."

Dr. Forsythe turned and grabbed his coat and briefcase and walked away to the door at the front of the class. People yelled out apologies for his son but he never looked at anyone and just held his hand up to wave us on.

"Oh my God," one kid said. "How devastating."

"Poor man," a girl said out loud.

Owen got up and went to the board outside. There was already a group of people looking and talking about the topic. Next to the list was a table with an instruction packet. Each student grabbed one. Owen looked at the packet and began reading:

Many Americans suffer from mental conditions. Here is a list of only a handful of those conditions. Look for your name on the board above and what condition you were assigned. There is no switching assignments. You are to write a paper on that condition. Each paper is to be typed, double-spaced, and no less than 50 pages. More instructions are available on my website. You may email me additional questions. I will be available to read your first ten pages in one week. This paper is worth 50% of your grade so I suggest you let me read the first ten pages to make sure you're on track. Good luck.

Owen looked up for his name. By his name, along with several other students, was the topic: Sociopath. "Ok," he thought. "I got this." This was actually a good thing since he could Google lots about sociopaths. He listened while others started announcing what they were writing about.

"Paranoid?"

"Borderline personality disorder. Oh great."

"Anyone wants to trade? What? We can't? Ugh…I got Obsessive Compulsive." "Narcissistic. Great I can write about my father."

Owen chuckled at all the comments. He was happy with his topic. He put the packet in his backpack and saw the elite make their way to the board.

"What did you get, Dawson?" a girl from the class who as infatuated with him asked.

"Sociopath," he replied in serious thought.

"Great," Owen thought.

"So did I, dude!" Sawyer high five him.

Lincoln glanced at the list. "Schizoid….ok." He nodded and took a picture of the list.

"I guess he needs that in case he forgets by the time he gets to his dorm," Owen said under his breath. Several students heard him and burst out laughing. The elite looked over at him. Owen grabbed his bag and headed to the library.

He began checking out as many books as allowed for his topic and put himself on the list for the ones he needed that someone had beaten him to. He sat in his usual spot and began reading and taking notes.

"I might as well just photocopy this entire book," he thought. "First, he would give the definition of the topic. History of sociopaths and famous people who have it. Diagnosis. Then what? That alone would take 10 pages, possibly 20. What would he write for the other thirty pages he needed?

He leaned back in his chair and sighed. This wasn't ideal. He looked across the room at the elite coming up the stairs. Usually noisy this time, they came up very quietly, looking behind them and around. They looked over at Owen where he was sitting; he pretended to stretch and looked away just in time.

They went over by a section of books. Aldridge stood outside the entry of section as if to keep anyone from entering. "Where are they buying drugs?" Owen thought for only a second. "No. They were jocks." He had watched them before. None of them smoked. They all ate healthy and worked out. That takes discipline.

Another student approached and Aldridge motioned him down the book section. The elite talked with him for about 30 seconds and each of them handed him their psychology packets, including Aldridge who took it out from his bag and handed it over without even turning around. He just kept watch. Then Dawson handed him a piece of paper. Sawyer, Lincoln, and Carson handed him cash. Carson came out and switched places with

Aldridge who then handed the student some cash. Then the student left and went to the bathroom and the elite left smiling.

Owen grabbed his book bag and went into the bathroom. The student, Earl Lee, nodded at him and washed his hands.

"What was that all about?" Owen asked.

"What are you talking about?" Earl asked nonchalantly.

"Did you sell them drugs or something?" Owen asked.

"No," Earl said and looked under the stalls. "What are you, some sort of nark?"

"No," Owen sighed. "I saw them give you their packets. Are they forcing you to write their papers or something?"

Earl laughed. "Dude, this isn't High School. They're paying me to write their papers. I'm good at it. I do this all the time. I write papers for a lot of students. Some people are good at sports but suck at papers. Some people have families and jobs and don't have time but need them to pass their course. I need a new car."

"What do you charge?" Owen asked.

Earl smiled. "Psychology or English?"

Owen responded," Psychology."

"How many pages?" Earl asked.

"50 pages on Sociopath," Owen replied.

Earl nodded. "The big one. $5000. Cash. $1000 down payment for the first ten pages."

"Are you serious?" Owen yelled.

"Dude, lower your voice. You don't have to buy the product if you don't like the price. I have plenty of clients. I could have it done in ten days for you. The whole paper. Up to you." Earl began combing his hair.

Owen grabbed his book bag and left the bathroom more mad then he had ever been in his life. Earl shrugged and yelled at him. "Realize this buddy, in the last five minutes I made $25000." Earl grinned at himself in the mirror.

Owen was not only mad but frustrated. He was here at this college because he worked hard in High School. Instead of drinking on weekends and drugging it up, he studied. He worked at his father's store and studied. He never missed any classes even coming in with a cold once and a fever. Other kids skipped classes if the weather was good.

He applied for colleges and won a scholarship. His parents had to pay for nothing. He did all the work. He had very little spending money and had to earn every grade. It pissed him off that others could just fork out cash and pay for their grades.

He slammed his book bag down on the table in the cafeteria and sat down and put his head in his hands and just sighed. "Um, this table is taken," a female told him. He looked up to see a group of girls. Another girl stood by the table, tray in hand, waiting to sit down. "Sorry," Owen said and quickly grabbed his stuff and left.

The elite watched and they all laughed except Dawson who saw his frustrations. "Knock it off, guys. He looks stressed," Dawson told them and they turned their attention back to their conversation.

Owen went back to his dorm room and threw his book bag across the room. Cliff wasn't there and wouldn't be for another two hours. Owen closed his eyes and fell asleep and missed the rest of his classes that day. It would be the first time he had missed classes ever.

CHAPTER 3
THE SUGGESTION

"Owen…. OWEN," Cliff shook him. Owen turned.

"What? What time is it?" Owen asked.

"It's 8 pm. Did you sleep all day?" Cliff asked.

"Oh my God," Owen sat up suddenly and closed his eyes. "I slept through three classes. I missed three classes."

"Calm down," Cliff reassured him. "Two of your teachers were out and the other one lasted ten minutes and dismissed the class. I think she had the flu or something. Just talk to the other students and see what you missed."

"I slept through dinner, too. Shit." Owen slapped his head.

"Good thing I was caller number seven," Cliff told him.

"What do you mean?" Owen asked, confused.

"Radio station had a contest for different stuff. DVD's, CD's, movie passes and pizza." Cliff explained as he held up several cards. "I was called number seven and we won 4 large pizzas. Hungry?"

Owen smiled and off they went to Pizza House which was a block off campus in the downtown district. It was a brisk walk but both of them were starving. Each coupon was a four-topping large and Cliff did a vegetarian and Owen a meat lovers delight. They each had water and sat down while their pizza was being prepared.

They could easily have taken it back to the dorm like so many college kids did or had it delivered but they needed to get away. Plus, hot pizza was the bomb. The place was full of High School kids and college kids. Plus, a few families.

It felt good to get away and Owen leaned back and sighed. "Rough day?" Cliff asked. Owen nodded and asked him how his classes were going. He then told him everything that happened that day.

"You want me to ask my dad for the money?" Cliff asked.

"No," Owen said bluntly. The thought had never crossed his mind and he would never even consider that.

"Good," Cliff explained. "He wouldn't give it to you anyway." They both laughed. Cliff came from a hard-working family. Like Owen, his family owned a store also. Five actually. All of them being laundromat businesses. The whole family worked there. Cousins too. Cliff was the first person from their family to go to college. Owen knew if he had to, Cliff could and would get the money from his parents. But to have hard-working people pay for his grades wasn't something he was willing to stoop to. He would just have to buckle down and do it the old-fashioned way and earn it.

"Besides," he thought. "He only had to make a C or better to maintain." His next paper was due soon so he had to just pump that one out. Everyone would get an A if there were no spelling errors and it was typed and double-spaced and on time. That would bring is grade back up to a C average. He relaxed some at this realization. He was going to be ok.

The guy's got back to the dorm after devouring two large pizzas. They decided to have the other two delivered to them the next day since it was the weekend. Cliff's Aunt was coming in on Sunday to spend the day with him and always brought food for the both of them which would last them two days. They could save their commissary money for junk food then.

Cliff planned to spend the whole Saturday playing videogames and taking one long shower. A day well spent. Owen decided to spend the day working on his first paper and then outlining the final one. Sunday would be spent doing the same thing and then taking a long shower. Most of the dorm went out on the weekends to visit family in the city so for those left, they utilized the shower time very well.

A student knocked on their door. "Hitting the shower for 30, is that ok?" he yelled.

"You're golden," Cliff yelled back.

"Thanks," the voice came back.

Cliff looked over at Owen. "When you're done with your first paper, I'll look it over before I leave so you can correct anything you missed."

"Thanks, dude." Owen smiled. He put on his sweats and hoodie and grabbed his book bag and headed out to the computer lab.

The weather was still chilled and light traces of snow were on the ground. He couldn't wait for spring. At least he didn't have to drive in this stuff. There were hardly any students out and only a few scattered in the cafeteria as he walked through. He passed the bowling alley and only one person was there. Inside the computer lab were about 8 students plugging away, each in their own world.

He grabbed a computer in the corner and set his area up and began. It was quiet in the room and all you could hear was the pounding of the keyboard. Now and then, someone would break the silence, asking how to spell a certain word or if there was a comma after something they wrote. He finished his paper in two hours. He spelled, checked it and then printed it.

"Don't forget to save it," a student reminded him. Owen nodded and turned back and grabbed a flash drive. As he saved it, he looked at the other papers people had written.

Someone had forgotten to clear their paper on Borderline personality. "Why couldn't it have been

Sociopath?" he thought. He read their outline which was about 14 pages. It was choppy but not bad. He sighed at the thought that this person was already this far ahead. He was about to erase it for that student but didn't since he wondered if he hadn't even saved it yet.

He didn't recognize the students' name but was sure he was probably in his class. He knew it wasn't one of the elites since they were all paying to have their papers done. He rolled his eyes and left for the library.

Inside the library, one of the staffers had brought homemade rice crispy treats. Most library ladies didn't like you eating in the library but most kids snuck in food anyway. The weekend lady didn't care.

"Would you like a treat?" she asked Owen. Owen smiled and nodded. He hadn't had one of these since his childhood. His expression showed that and she smiled. "Take a few more. I made a lot," she whispered and he nodded. He walked upstairs as another student walked in and she offered him some too. He also took some.

Owen sat down and began working on his paper. He worked on it all afternoon and into the evening. He finally stopped because the library was about to close and about the same time, Cliff texted him the pizza was on the way. Even though he had just had pizza yesterday, the sound of hot pizza was just too good to pass up. He packed up and put his papers in his back pack and put his books back and headed back to the dorm.

He passed a lot of kids going to the football field. He hadn't been to a game yet but wasn't even interested. All he cared about was his paper. He had heard the school was ranked in the top 3 but again, he didn't care.

He walked in just as the pizza guy was leaving. "Cheap tip," he muttered and Owen smiled. It wasn't as if they ordered pizza every week.

He entered the room and the aroma got to him. Suddenly, the paper meant nothing to him. All that mattered was that pizza. His was on his bed and Cliff was still playing videogames and had a slice hanging out of his mouth. He swallowed and looked over at Owen. "How is the paper coming?" he asked.

"First one done and ready for a look over. Second one is slowly being outlined," he replied.

"I'll look it over before I leave tomorrow morning," Cliff reminded him.

"Ok. Thanks. Thanks for the pizza also," Owen said as he stuffed his face.

The next day, Aunt Vivian arrived and whisked Cliff away. As usual, she invited Owen but he reclined. She dropped off food and promised to bring more when she brought Cliff back. Cliff found only one mistake on Owen's paper but that one mistake would cost him a letter grade.

He ate the food she brought and then went to the computer lab and made the correction. He reprinted his paper and typed out the big one. He printed it out and had only 17 pages. "Not bad for the first attempt," he thought, but how in the heck was he going to come up with another 33 pages?

He decided to take a break from the madness and play some videogames. He would schedule a time for Dr. Forsythe to read his paper and go from there. He headed back to the dorm and ran into an over-excited student.

"Did you hear?" he smiled, running out the door.

"What's going on?" Owen asked.

"Our college was chosen for a free movie at the theater in town today. All students who show their name badge get in free for any movie!" he yelled.

"Cool. Don't have a car," Owen shrugged.

"The school is letting us use the bus to and back, man. The bus will run every two hours until 1000," the student added.

Owen nodded. He could use the break. He ran upstairs and threw his book bag on the bed and headed back downstairs. He ran outside and inside the bus just as it closed the doors. Within a 40-minute drive, he was at the front of the movie theater with 28 other students and surrounded by others from the college who had cars.

He got in and sat down at the first movie that was available and smiled. He was pleased with himself. He had finished his one paper and he managed to at least outline the first 17 pages. He would show it to the teacher and go from there. He did it in two days and on his own and it didn't cost him thousands of dollars. Owen smiled and enjoyed the day.

Two movies later, it was close to 9 pm. He had found a half-eaten tub of popcorn and an empty soda cup which was large. That meant free refill on both. So, he cleaned them out and went up to the counter and refilled everything. Others might consider that cheap but he considered it thrifty. Full on popcorn and soda, he headed outside to wait for the bus who showed up an hour later. He listened while others complained about teachers, roommates, dorms and papers graded unfairly.

The ride home was nauseating because he chose to sit in the back and the city had never repaired the pot holes. The driver made it a goal to hit everyone. Once inside the dorm, Cliff had just arrived himself and was bummed; he missed out on free movies all day and instead went to see flower gardens at the city center with his aunt instead.

He had brought Owen sweat-pulled pork from the restaurant his Aunt took him to but Owen was exhausted from relaxing all day and full of popcorn. He promised to eat it for breakfast and soon both men were fast asleep.

The next day, Owen put his paper in the basket on the desk in front of the class and then signed up for a meeting with Dr. Forsythe from the options available on the forms he had left on the desk. There was no class for a week so he headed to the library and started trying to come up with any idea on how to fill another 33 pages of information for his paper.

He saw Earl making more connections in the library and thought how easy it would be to get him expelled and so many more but then thought, what good would that do? What would it accomplish? How would that make him look to the rest of the school?

He continued day dreaming until his next class. By the end of the day, he had caught up on every class project except the big one. Basically, that's all he had left to work on. Finish the paper and he was done for the year. He sat up in his chair and smiled. Not bad. He would have year one done.

He'd go to his parents' house in the summer and work for his dad in the store and he'd see how serious he was. Maybe Cliff and him could be dorm roommates again the following year. He looked down at his watch. His meeting with Dr. Forsythe was only two days away. He had signed up for the second day of meetings since no one else had. He didn't want to seem over-exuberant.

Finally, the day came and he walked into the hallway. There were three other students there. You were expected to wait in the hall until the first student came out. Dr. Forsythe was already inside talking with a girl.

"Are you Riley?" a male student asked. Owen nodded. "Then you're up next and then her and then me. I just didn't want to be late and I was hoping one of you wouldn't show."

You didn't want to come late to anything assigned to this class. You followed all the mundane instructions and didn't even talk unless spoken to in class. Owen was eager to see what the teacher had to say about his paper. "What a boring job to be a teacher," Owen thought. All those papers. Finally, the girl came out looking defeated.

"Asshole," she muttered.

"Next student," Dr. Forsythe's voice bellowed from inside.

Everyone looked at Owen and he walked in. He came down the carpeted area and sat at the chair placed for them. He opened his book bag and looked at Dr. Forsythe who was watching him intently. Like he was figuring him out.

Dr. Forsythe looked drained and depressed which was understandable for the situation he was going through.

"Thank you for seeing me today, Dr. Forsythe and I'm very sorry for your loss sir," Owen said quietly.

"Thank you, Mr. Riley," Dr. Forsythe held out his hand for his paper. "I gave you an A for your last paper. Good thing you listened to my instructions. So many didn't. You were only one of twelve A's I gave for a simple paper."

Owen sighed in relief. Dr. Forsythe watched him and then read his paper. He circled words and wrote on the side of the paper comments which was good. Owen wanted his opinion on everything. It took about a good 15 minutes and Owen said nothing but watched him. Several times, a student would peek in to see if someone was actually down in the classroom.

Dr. Forsythe then handed him the paper back. "How many pages so far?" he asked.

"Seventeen sir," Owen announced.

"Not bad for the first two days. You're further than most. You have the content. Make those corrections and blow me out of the water with the rest and you'll ace this class. You're on track, Mr. Riley. Have a nice day," Dr. Forsythe looked away.

Owen smiled and stood up. "Thank you, sir. Thank you." He grabbed his bag and walked away immediately, giving another student a chance to come down right away. Outside in the hallway, he read all the comments.

Owen's enthusiasm turned to sadness almost immediately. He shot down something in every paragraph on every page. He wrote words like: Predictable. Paraphrasing. Too wordy. Lame sample. More content. Boring. Cliché.

Owen was back at square one but he wasn't too disappointed. He learned that he still had a C in the class. He was only one of a handful of students who had gotten an A on the last paper and he was further than others on this paper and he was on track. He just needed to make corrections and come up with a way to blow Dr. Forsythe out of the water.

Owen laughed and headed back to the dorm. Cliff was working on his assignment at the time. Owen showed him the paper and told him everything that Dr. Forsythe had to say. Then, they both played videogames the rest of the day.

After dinner, Owen stared blankly at the computer screen in his room. He had no ideas and he was feeling very frustrated. After about the fourth sigh, Cliff looked over at him. "Why don't you just go into a chat room and ask if there are any sociopaths there and interview them?"

Owen looked at Cliff and laughed. They both laughed for a good thirty seconds. "Do you think that would work?

"Why not?" Cliff asked. "It's worth a try."

"Where would I go?" Owen was intrigued.

Cliff thought a moment. "Go to the Vibe. It's a city chat room and it's free for everyone and everyone goes to talk about politics, religion, education, to each other. They talk about everything."

"So, I just go on and ask any sociopaths in the room?" Owen asked, laughing.

Cliff nodded. "Why not?"

"Because it's stupid. It's weird. It's not going to work." Owen announced.

"How do you know?" Cliff asked.

Owen stared at him for about thirty seconds. "I mean, you're right. Why not?" Cliff nodded and shrugged in agreement. "I could use a different name, right?" Owen asked. Cliff shook his head no.

"I wouldn't do that," he told Owen. "Think about it. You'll probably tell him you're a student and you need to interview a sociopath but if you lie and you meet him someday, he's going to be pissed. I would just use your name and if you Skype with him, cool. If you meet him then meet him in a local well-populated area like a mall or a busy restaurant."

"Ok," Owen got excited. "Let's do this."

CHAPTER 4
A BITE OF THE APPLE

Owen took a deep breath. For some reason, he changed shirts before he sat down to go onsite. It was as if he was dressing up for an interview. He had a notepad and pen next to him. His cell phone was fully charged. He had a list of notes on the left of the computer and a bottle of water. He was ready.

Cliff told him how to get online to the chat room and he began. He entered the room and announced himself to everyone. Many people said hi to him. One person asked his age and another if he was gay or straight. Cliff reassured him those were normal things people would ask to see who they were talking with.

"Keep in mind everyone in the room is blind here. No one knows who's on the other side of the keyboard so you have to give them something and not be upset over the questions," Cliff explained.

"I'm a straight college student looking to have someone help me with a paper I have to write," he wrote.

"What's your name, honey," a woman named Alice asked.

"Ahh straight? Bummer." a man named Big Bob wrote.

"John here and the topic is homeless people in the city and what we can do about it," John added.

"My name is Owen and I'm a psychology major and I have to write a huge paper on Sociopaths and was wondering if there are any out there and would they be willing to let me interview them for my paper?" Owen wrote.

"I love your name, Owen honey," Alice wrote.

"Down girl. He's a college student," Big Bob wrote.

"They have to learn somehow," Alice wrote.

Owen laughed. "Omg, these people are something else," he thought.

"Mary here and you should talk to my ex-husband or any of his family. They're all sociopaths," Mary added to the conversation.

"Don't sociopaths usually not recognize they are sociopaths?" another man in the room named Mike wrote.

"I think they do but won't admit it or they have been told they are by someone else. So, if you fall into this category or know someone who does, I will leave my email at the end of this note so you can contact me," Owen wrote and added his email address.

"I hope you changed your name to protect yourself," Archie, another person on the line, added.

"Yes, honey," Alice wrote. "You don't know the weirdos out there.

"Anyone of us could be a nut job." Big Bob wrote. Everyone responded.

Lol

LOL

LMFAO

LOL

Lol

"I'm willing to take a chance to get my paper done." Owen writes. Small talk continues as Owen slowly feels he's made a big mistake. Owen shakes his head as talk moves from his paper back to the homeless issue. "This is like fishing in an empty lake," he mutters. He sighs and suddenly gets an instant message.

Owen sits up and stares at the upper right corner of his computer. "Who would be messaging him?" He suddenly gets clarity. It had to be someone from the room. He looked at the names. The same people were talking however there were over 40 people in the room but not engaging in the format. Just observing. He smiled.

Owen clicked the message.

"How serious are you?"

Owen sighed and smiled. He was ready. He answered. "I'm very serious. I need to write an awesome paper to stay in this program. I would love to interview a sociopath and I would be willing to let you read the paper before even turning it in. I'll even change the names, of course so no one knows who it's about."

Owen sat back and waited.

"That would defeat the purpose of the world knowing who we are. Wouldn't it?"

Owen read and chuckled. "Oh my God," he thought. "He's a sociopath. I'm writing with a sociopath." The messenger wrote again.

"Who knows…. maybe we'll let you join our club."

"Club?" Owen's eyes widened. "They have a club of sociopaths?" He smiled. He wrote back. "I wish I could meet all of you. Do you think that could happen?"

"Be careful about what you wish for, Owen."

Owen chuckled. He glanced over at his notes. Something he circled stood out. He read it. "How to spot a sociopath."

* Superficial Charm

* Absence of delusions

* Unreliability

* Insincerity

* Lack of remorse

* Lying

He glanced away from his notes and turned them over. He stared at his "D" paper. He began to type. "I'm ready to take a bite of the apple. Even if the apple is poisoned." He hit "enter" and sat back and waited. A few seconds went by.

"Corner of Tyler and 14th street. 8 p.m. sharp."

"What is this place? Is it where you all hang out?" Owen typed.

"No, Owen. It's a neutral place we can meet for the first time."

Owen sighed. "What should I call you?"

"My name is Archie. I'll be in one of the booths."

Owen nodded. "What will you be wearing?" Owen waited but got no more responses from Archie. He looked at all the names of everyone in the room. Many were leaving so he quickly scrolled. No one was named Archie. He didn't care. He made contact with a real sociopath and tonight, he would meet him. Owen googled the address and it was a diner.

"Cool," he thought. "I'll have dinner with a sociopath and write my paper based on our conversation. I'll even call it that." Owen brought up his paper on the computer. "My dinner with a sociopath." He laughed.

Owen leaned back in his chair and looked at his wardrobe. "What do you wear to dinner with a sociopath?" He stood up and started looking at his wardrobe. The door suddenly opened and Cliff stood there.

"Dude it worked," Owen told him everything. Cliff sat on the bed, listening intently. "Don't sociopaths not believe they are sociopaths?" Cliff asked, trying to understand this all.

"I think so. Yeah." Owen said without hesitation.

"Well, if that's true why is he meeting you?" Cliff asked.

"Dude, why the questions?" Owen yelled.

"No I mean," Cliff thought. "Look, just be careful. You don't know anything about this guy."

"I'm sorry. I know. And you're right. Sociopaths don't believe they are sociopaths. Maybe this one is more intelligent. Maybe he came to grips with it after being diagnosed and he wants to help others. I don't know. We're meeting at a dinner in the city. So, it's out in the open." Owen reassured his concerned roommate.

Cliff nodded. "Just don't go anywhere with him afterwards."

"Ok Dad," Owen laughed. Cliff laughed. Owen held up two shirts. "Which one should I wear to dinner?"

"What do you wear to meet a sociopath?" Cliff asked. "Do certain colors trigger them or something?"

Owen thought and shook his head no. "I just want to look good." Cliff nodded and turned away. Owen laughed and got dressed.

CHAPTER 5
DINNER WITH A SOCIOPATH

Owen stared at the diner from across the street. He surveyed the area carefully. The diner was an old train cart turned into a restaurant. He could see people inside sitting when the door opened. The windows were too small to look into from outside. He looked around and took a deep breath. He thought of his grade and his parents and nodded. He was going in. He made the decision to go in.

He started across the street and reached for the door handle. He looked around one more time and sighed. "It's a frigging interview Owen," he thought to himself. "You can leave anytime you feel uncomfortable and just wing it from there. Get enough to get your paper done." He nodded and walked in.

He glanced around the diner. The cash register was right in front and on the left-hand side was the kitchen for the cooks and a line of bar stools for those who wanted to sit at the counter. On the right side was a line of booths. He counted seven and three at the back where there was a bathroom everyone could use in the far left back.

He glanced at all the booths. All of them were occupied. One had a woman alone. Two had couples. The other four had one person sitting at each one. All men.

"Honey, just sit where you want and I'll come find you." the waitress smiled at him from behind the counter. He nodded. One of the men got up to leave, grabbing his ticket. "Ok, so it wasn't him. That left three options," he thought to himself.

"Archie, you need another coffee honey?" the waitress yelled across the room. Owen looked as a man in the next to the last booth raised his cup. His eyes were on Owen and their eyes met. Owen nodded and so did Archie.

"Ok this is good," Owen thought. "He showed up. His name was Archie. He was surrounded by others. What did he have to lose?" Owen walked up to the table and held out his hand for Archie.

"Hello, Archie. My name is Owen Riley."

Archie shook his hand. "Hello, Owen Riley. Sit down and let's talk." Owen smiled and sat down. "Coffee?" Archie asks and holds his hand up to the waitress. Alice!" Owen shakes his head no.

"Tea please, Iced." Owen asks.

Archie nods. "Alice, an iced tea for Owen Riley here."

"Lemon in that tea, Owen Riley?" Alice asks. She stands tall in her high heels. Her hair is done in a Bee Hive like from the 1950s and her makeup is caked on.

"No, thank you." Owen smiles. He wonders how she can work for hours in those heels as he stares at them. Archie follows his eyes and smiles.

"Did you bring your paper?" Archie asks.

"No Sir," Owen turns back to him, giving him full attention. "I thought we'd talk and then I'd write it and then show it to you if that's ok?"

Archie smiles. "It's ok." Archie is wearing a suit a businessman would be wearing.

He's about 5 foot 10 and around 175 pounds. He looks retired but might be in his 60s. Owen doesn't see a wedding ring but eyeballs everything about him. Archie knows what he's doing and they share a quiet moment while he lets Owen take everything in. "We have to rules." Archie breaks the silence.

"Rules?" Owen asks, curious.

"Yes," Archie responds quickly. "Society is built on rules. First, don't call me sir. Call me Archie. Second, honesty is key. No lies. Third, I get to read your paper when it's done first before your teacher. Don't worry, it will be quick. If I don't like it, you have to change it. If you don't change it then I keep the paper."

Owen thinks. "No problem."

"Ok." Archie nods. "I see you brought paper and pen. Are you going to take notes?" "Yes Sir…I mean, yes Archie." Owen corrects himself.

Archie nods. "Good." Alice arrives with the tea and Archie and Alice exchange a look as Owen begins pulling out his pen and paper. He writes the time and date as Archie watches him.

"Bye, Bob. Have a good day, Hun." Alice remarks as he leaves. Bob, a heavy-set man wearing a city lime green safety vest, waves and leaves.

"Ok, so tell me about you," Owen asks.

"Tell me about you first Owen," Archie asks. "Who is Owen Riley? Who is interviewing me?"

Owen nods. "Trust. Gotcha." He looks around. "I'm from Chewelah, a small town a few hours away from Spokane. I'm the oldest of five kids and my parents own a small store. My parents wanted me to stay there and run the store. Get married. Stay there." Archie smiles as Owen continues. "My father was disappointed I went to college and he's more disappointed I'm taking psychology. My mother has adapted. I'm finishing up my first year if I get this paper done. I'm single and there are no prospects in my future and I have a pet lizard named Frank. And a roommate named Cliff."

"Riveting," Archie comments. Owen nods. "I know. I know." They both laugh.

"My name is Archie. I'm a lawyer. A divorce lawyer." Archie begins. "I've been married four times. Divorced three times. One died. I have 2 kids. I never see them. They've washed their hands off me. I guess mainly because I put my career first and them second and my wives third. So, when I did pay off the house and the lake property and put them in brand-new cars on their 16th birthday, they didn't have time for me. I missed everything. Holidays, birthdays, school events. Everything. Now they're both married and have kids and I haven't even met my grandkids. I think I have three. Last I heard.

Not sure."

Owen nods. "I'm sorry?"

"Why?" Archie asks. Owen shrugs. "Don't ever be sorry. It was my decision. My life. My choices. I own them."

"Yes, sir." Owen closes his eyes. "Sorry." Sighs.

Archie laughs. "Was your dad in the military?"

"No." Owen responds.

"Was he a strict southern?" Archie asks.

"Kind of." Owen laughs. "My grandparents were from the South."

"That explains the sir." Archie grins. "What are your grades in school?"

"In most of my classes, good. In psychology, I am hanging on by a thread. I need to write the most amazing paper and blow my teacher's mind." Owen explains.

Archie smiles. "I know how you can do that."

Owen smiles. "By letting me write about you?"

Archie shakes his head no. "By letting you write about all of us."

Owen sits up and straightens himself up. He grabs two sugars and prepares his tea. He drinks a sip. "All of you?" Owen finally breaks the silence.

"The whole club," Archie announces.

"There's a club?" Owen asks.

"The Sociopath Club," Archie says bluntly.

Owen looks around to see if anyone hears. He's blown away by this revelation. Archie smiles at his response.

"Let me get this straight," Owen whispers. "You're telling me that there is a club of sociopaths who meet ….as a club….. and do what?"

Archie shrugs his shoulders. "Drink. Play cards. Converse. Scheme. What do people usually do at clubs?"

Owen places both hands on his head and his mouth falls open. "I'm blown away. Dude, this is crazy. I mean…. poor choice of words but you're telling me you belong to a club that only has sociopaths and you're going to let me come and meet them and write about them?"

Archie leans forward. "I have to ask them first. But I don't see a problem. Our egos are pretty big."

"Do you think they'll let me come? Why would they?" Owen asks.

"Well, I think they'll say yes because you would be showing the world….by your paper…. that our kind is misunderstood or maybe we just think we are. Or maybe your paper will show a little insight into our kind. Either way, a room full of future psychiatrists will know about us. Be more open to us. It's a win-win situation. You get your paper written and blow your teacher's mind by not only writing about one sociopath but a club of them and we are more understood or the world is aware of us." Archie leans back.

Owen leans back. "Why me? I thought sociopaths didn't realize they were sociopaths?"

Archie smiles. "Because you asked. Yes, in the beginning, sociopaths don't realize they are. It takes years of convincing and sit-downs at the doctor's office but then you realize you're not the problem but the solution, and you find others or run into them and realize you're not alone anymore. You decide to find a place all of you can meet in case you run into others. Word of mouth, clients, neighbors, etc.....and soon you have your own club. A place we can meet and be ourselves to talk, play cards, drink, socialize and help each other with problems."

Owen nods. "Do you think they'll be open to me?"

Archie smiles and stands up. He places the money on the table. "Give me your phone number. To text only. Wait for my text." Owen looks around and writes it down on the paper he brought and hands it to Archie. Archie puts it in his pocket. "I think they'll love it. For some, it will be a game. For others, a stage to showcase their opinions of the world and for some enlightenment. A way for the world to see that we are not invisible. How you find us will reflect on your paper. That will be the true test of friendship."

Archie leaves as Owen stays sitting in shock.

CHAPTER 6
THE SOCIOPATH CLUB

Owen ran back into his room full of excitement. "Dude, wake up. Wake up. I have so much to tell you."

Cliff wakes and Owen tells him everything. "Are you sure this is a good idea? I mean, you really don't know anything about him." Cliff explains.

"He's been married four times. Three of his wives are alive and well and one died. He's probably divorced because he is a sociopath and they probably figured it out. The other one died because …I don't know…natural causes. Or maybe he killed her. Do sociopaths kill? Anyway…he has kids, grandkids and he's a lawyer which is a popular job trait among sociopaths." Owen says, leaning back in his computer chair.

"What's his last name?" Cliff asks. Owen shrugs. "Where is his office?" Cliff asks another question. Owen shrugs. "So where is this club at?" Cliff asks once more.

"Look, I don't know. It was our first meeting. I don't even know if they'll say yes for me to come interview them." Owen fires back.

Cliff sighs. "They'll say yes. I guarantee it. They're sociopaths. They live for this stuff. They're like drugs. You'll go there and fall in love with them. Try it once and you'll be hooked. I'm telling you, dude. Drop this. Just make shit up and write your paper. Maybe interview someone from the jail? Or call a psychiatric office and have him print your shit off. Anything but this. You're playing with fire."

"Well, I love pyromania!" Owen laughs. He continues. "You're the one who suggested I do this." Cliff looks serious. "I'll be fine, dude. But this is the only way. I already printed off everything about sociopaths from the Library. I called the jail and they wouldn't grant me clearance. I even asked a psychiatric doctor if I could be in the room with one of their clients who was a sociopath and they said no way it was a breach of ethics and it broke the client privacy law. This is my paper. I'm doing it."

Cliff nods. "Ok, dude. I got your back. Just be careful, ok?" Owen nods. "Just when you leave and go there, leave me a text or note so I know when you leave. I doubt if they'll let you tell me where you are so just be careful."

"I will." Owen sighs and begins to write his notes on Archie. He looks over at the table and eyeballs a phone book. Cliff goes to bed as Owen dims the light and goes to the Yellow Pages. He looks up attorney's and goes through every one of them. Within an hour, he's done and he leans back and sighs. "Not one of them is named Archie," he whispers and looks at his roommate. He looks over at his parents' picture and then at his last assignment. He outlines the D on the page and smiles. "I'm doing this."

His phone goes off and he looks at the new message. It's from Archie. It reads:

Meet and greet

14th and Grant

5 pm sharp.

Bring chips and dip.

A.

Owen rereads the message five more times. He smiles. He texts back, "I'll be there. Thanks." He looks over at his closet. "What do you wear to a meet and greet with sociopaths?" he laughs.

Next day, Owen stands outside 14th and Grant. It's 4:55. He's holding a bowl of chips and has a bag in his other hand. He looks at the apartment building. This makes no sense. It's an apartment building. He looks around the left side and around but nothing sparks. He looks toward his right and he sees a mailman going down a stairway where there is a red door. He places the mail there and leaves. Owen goes down the stairs and, on the mailbox, it reads:

THE S.P. CLUB

He smiles. He looks at the red door for a moment. There is no peephole. There is no door knocker. On the top of the door is a brass "22." "That's odd," he thinks. He rings the bell and steps a bit back. The door opens suddenly and a man stands there.

"Hi, my name is Owen. I was invited." Owen stands still. The man looks him up and down and stops at the chips. The man burst out laughing and steps aside to let him in.

"Well, hello Owen. We've been expecting you. And you brought chips and I'm assuming that's dip in the bag?" the man asks. Owen nods and then realizes he's the butt of their joke. This was an initiation on sociopaths and knowing not to upset them, he nods and holds it up.

"Hi, I'm Owen and I brought the chips and dip." He announces to the room full of people.

Everyone laughs and claps. He's in. He knows it. He passed the first test. Archie walks over, holding a cigar and a shot glass. Archie hugs Owen and starts introducing him to everyone.

"Owen, this is McCallister. Best dentist in the city." Archie announces.

"How do you do?" Owen shakes his hand.

"This is Rio. He works in the factory in town," Archie explains.

"Pleasure to meet you Owen," Rio shakes his hand.

"Pleasure to meet you Rio," Owen smiles.

"This is Claudia. She's a bartender on the north side." Archie explains.

"Pleasure to meet you, Claudia." Owen nods.

"What a gentleman. What a change." Claudia announces out loud and is met with a room full of laughter.

"This is Baker. He's a chef." Archie explains.

Owen shakes his hands and is then introduced to Wrangler, dressed in jeans with a bolo tie, cowboy hat, and boots. He meets Rhett who comes across as a perfectionist in his neatly pressed suit and tie and greased down hair.

"Everett is an officer of the law and Francine is a judge," Archie explains as they all shake hands. He continues introducing Owen to others. "Candice is a teacher and Nelson is in construction. Finally, this is Father Francis." They both shake hands. Archie looks around the room. "That's the ones that are here right now. You'll meet the others at other times." He looks at Owen's hands. "I can't believe you really brought chips and dip." Owen bursts out laughing and so does Archie.

They order drinks and sit at a table. Everyone goes back to their business except Nelson who joins Archie and Owen.

"Thank you again for letting me come here and be a part of all of this," Owen says, looking around the room. The room is done very richly with oak and leather and green and black accents. Brass is outlined around the room. A lot of money went into the room's décor.

"You're not in just yet," Nelson announces. Owen looks at him and he shakes his head, Owen. "Not yet. You have to prove yourself."

"Prove myself? For what?" says Owen.

"Attitude, boy." Nelson sets up to show his dominance. Archie holds his hand up to Owen and then pushes Nelson back.

"Watch your ego. He's new. He doesn't understand. We have to only explain it to him."

Archie calmly responds to them both. Nelson looks away at the mirror and fixes his hair. He notices that Owen is watching him and turns back to glare at him. Owen shows no reaction and looks at Archie.

Calmly Owen asks, "How do I prove myself to all of you?"

"A sign of a sociopath is our lack of shame. Our calm during circumstances. How we are known to manipulate or exploit someone who has done us wrong? This is how we initiate others into our club. You want to be a part of our society; you have to show us we can trust you. You are to go out and hurt someone. Not kill them. But emotionally hurt someone who has harmed you. Then you're in." Archie explains and sits back.

Owen looks from Archie to Nelson and then around the room which is now eerily quiet. All eyes are on him.

"Or," Nelson leans forward. "You can leave now. Pretend you never came here."

Owen thinks what Cliff said about being in this situation. Owen looks at Archie and leans over to Nelson. "I'm in," he announces and everyone cheers.

Owen leans back and looks at Archie. "How will you know I did anything?" Owen asks.

"It will be all over your face," Archie announces.

"Run along boy and get it done." Nelson points to the door. Owen looks at Archie who looks away. Owen knows the meet and greet was officially at the end. This whole charade was to see if he'd really walk through the door and make the commitment. It was also a way for everyone to see him. What they didn't know was how committed he was.

Owen was ready for this challenge. He had been inside the secret society and he wanted in further. He wanted to interview every person he had met today and no matter what initiation they had in mind, he was ready for it.

Owen walked to the door and looked at the man who had let him in. "You should really get a peephole for that door. You never know who you're letting in."

The man smiled. "Not afraid of what's outside in the world. I would be more concerned about what's inside."

He raced home and wrote all his notes down and then typed them up. The description of the room. Everyone's name and title and the initiation he was expected to do. When Cliff arrived, he caught him up to speed.

Cliff pointed out that he didn't text him where he was going and that what he was doing was dangerous. He also pointed out that once again, he only had first names and no last names to go on.

"I still know their jobs," Owen reassured him.

"Yes that's true," Cliff said sarcastically. "You know Nelson, the construction worker and Claudia…what was she…oh yeah, a bartender."

"Ok I get your point," Owen remarked.

"Do you?" Cliff stood firm. "I looked in the yellow pages of all the attorneys in town. No Archie's are attorneys."

"I know I did the same after you fell asleep," Owen replied. Cliff sighed.

Owen went online and googled "Judges" in the city.

"What are you doing?" Cliff asked.

"Here," Owen said excitedly. "Here is one of them. Judge Francine McKenzie. Look, I met her."

Cliff examines her picture and nods. "Ok, but please just be careful. These people all have psychiatric issues and we don't know what they're capable of."

Owen nods. "They um…. they want to initiate me into the club."

Cliff turns around. "What? Why?"

Owen looks up at the ceiling and then looks at Cliff. "They want to see if they can trust me first. So, they want me to hurt someone who hurt me or made me mad. Not kill them just hurt them, and then I'm in and I can interview them and get my paper done."

Cliff stares at him. "Are you kidding me? Do you know how stupid this all sounds? Do you understand how dangerous this is? This isn't a game. What if something goes wrong? Why would you even need to do all this? Why not just interview them and leave?"

Owen shrugs. "Their society. Their rules."

Cliff's mouth falls open. "Society? I thought it was a club. Now you're saying society. I think they're pulling you in dude."

Owen shakes his head and then shrugs. "I don't see the harm. All I see is the end result. Me getting a psychiatric degree and becoming a doctor. I need this paper."

Cliff points at him. "At what cost? Do you even hear yourself talking here? At what costs? Their entertainment? For an A? To impress the teacher? Your parents? To lose your soul? If they ask you to jump off the top of a bridge, are you going to do that, too? "Dude, you're going a bit off target there with that. I'm not killing anyone." Owen reminds him.

"This time. This semester. What if next semester, your topic is Serial Killers? Are you going to join their club and kill someone for initiation?" Cliff grabs his jacket and leaves.

Owen thinks for a moment and looks out the window. He sees Dawson ride up on his motorcycle. He gets off and checks on the locks on the car next to his bike. "A BMW and a motorcycle," Owen shakes his head. "Lucky son of a bitch."

Owen turns and walks away and then looks back at the bike and car and smiles. He walks over to his closet and shakes his head. He looks over at Cliff's clothes and grabs his black hoodie and puts it on. He leaves and goes outside.

Chapter 7
Playing with Fire

Owen knew where the security cameras were. He glanced over at the counter and slowly walked behind, making sure no one could see his face or him. Whoever was supposed to be on duty was in the bathroom so time was limited. He grabbed the plug and unplugged it and headed outside.

Outside, Owen quickly undid the bolts on the wheels of Dawson's car. He goes back inside and quickly throws the hoodie into the laundry room. He goes back into his room and goes to sleep.

The next morning, Owen goes to class. He glances over at Dawson who is talking with several girls. Dawson eyeballs another girl in class who has a camera on her desk and begins asking her questions about her camera.

She blows him off which intrigues him even more. His friends pull him back but Owen can tell he's getting tired of their company and wants another life beyond adoring girls and football.

Class goes on as usual and as they get up to leave, the friend of the girl whispers to Dawson that they're going on a photo shoot on top of Long Lake. Dawson smiles and nods. Owen looks over at him.

"Dr. Forsythe?" Lincoln raises his hand.

"Yes?" Dr. Forsythe asks.

"Where do we put our finished papers?" Lincoln asks, holding up a massive paper.

"You're done?" Dr. Forsythe asks.

Lincoln nods. "So am I sir," Carson adds. Owen looks over as all of them, Dawson included have their papers. Owen bites his tongue as others in the class groan.

"Amazing that all five of the football team have their papers done during football season, ahead of schedule and on the same day," Dr. Forsythe announces. Some class members laugh.

"I told you guys to hand them in on different days," Dawson whispers. Owen shakes his head.

The guys strut out as the rest of the class leaves. Owen glares at Dawson as he follows his friends out the door to their next class.

"Dawson! Dawson!" a girl runs by Owen. Owen could smell her perfume. It smelled like spring and sunshine.

"Who was she?" he wondered. She stopped running and turned back around.

"Boys!" she rolled her eyes at Owen and smiled. "Hi."

"Hi," he smiled back and suddenly the halls were full of students and she was lost in the crowd but etched in Owen's memory.

Owen went back to his room and worked on his paper and then played videogames with Cliff. Owen fantasized about the girl and kept checking his phone every five minutes. No messages from Archie. A knock at the door broke the fantasy.

"Guys, Myers got a DVD player from his parents, were setting it up in the day room and watching Halloween. Come on," a random from the building yelled. He then went to the next room and the next.

Cliff and Owen headed downstairs to join the others. Someone else ran to the store and got a few more DVD rentals and everyone chipped in a few bucks for pizza and soon the party was on. Before they knew it - it was midnight and everyone headed to bed or to another party at a different building.

Owen walked into class and threw his books on the desk. He sighed still tired from the night before. Dr. Forsythe locked the door and headed down to the front of the room as several people beaded on the door. Owen glanced at the door and then over at Dawson and his crew. The crew was there but Dawson was nowhere in sight.

"How's Dawson doing? Any word?" a girl asked Aldridge. He shrugged but it got Owen's attention.

"What happened?" Owen asked. The crew saw his concern.

"We don't know. His tire came off yesterday when he was driving. He crashed," Sawyer responded.

"What?" Owen said in disbelief. He remembered he loosened them but just to make them wobbly. He didn't think he undid the whole thing. Or maybe he did.

"Has he woken up yet?" another asked.

The guys shook their heads. "The doctor said he had a concussion and a broken arm and busted up knee. He's out for the season." Carson responded.

"That means he misses out on the scholarship and he loses his spot on the team." Aldridge added.

"It also means he has to take the whole year over, too," Carson added.

Owen sat back for the rest of the class time. He never took notes. It was as if time stood still. Everything moved but him. When class ended, he got up and collected his books.

He glanced at his phone and looked at the message.

You're in. See you this weekend at the club. 0900.

A.

Owen sat back down and closed his eyes. No one was supposed to get hurt. He must have gone up to the lake and on the way down, the tire came off. He listened to all the gossip that day in the library and in the common room and in the halls. He learned that Dawson was up on the hill and on the way down, his tire came undone. He was going pretty fast and lost control while trying to adjust. He went off a small embankment and hit a tree.

The girl and her friends who he went up to see, came down not long after him and saw the car and called for help.

Owen went back to the dorm. As he headed back, he passed the Dean and Dawson's parents. They were arguing with the Dean but the Dean didn't back down. Owen kept his distance. One of the students was talking as they went by and said "I guess money can't buy everything."

The parents must have been trying to salvage the year for Dawson. But the Dean didn't bend the rules for them. The father looked very upset but the mom seemed to already move on.

Owen called all the hospitals and decided to visit Dawson. There was one more quarter and Dawson had already turned in his assignments for this quarter in his first class so he should be able to pass that class. Maybe he was set up for his other classes already. Maybe his father didn't know that. He could tell him.

Owen walked into the dorm room just as a hoodie came flying across the room, hitting him in the face. "What did you do?" Cliff yelled.

"What are you talking about?" Owen asked.

"My hoodie was downstairs in the laundry room. I know I left it here." Cliff yelled.

"Maybe you left it down in the lobby last night when we watched the movie and someone just put it there?" Owen tried to cover up.

"No, I didn't. I remember what I wear from day to day, Owen," Cliff yelled. "Besides, someone saw someone in a black hoodie messing around with Dawson's car. They went down to investigate."

"And?" Owen started to sweat.

"Well, nothing." Cliff responded. "But he crashed and I know you had to do something to someone who hurt you or you didn't like. I know you don't care for Dawson and his crew… hell no one does. What did you do?"

"You're right; lots of people don't like him. It could have been anyone." Owen thought.

"Stop it, Owen." Cliff pushes him out of his train of thought. "You're becoming like them. Just to join them."

"No, I'm not." Owen started to see a similar pattern of thought.

"What did you do?" Cliff asks again.

"I loosened some bolts on his car," Owen said quietly.

"That shouldn't have made his tire come off. Are you sure you didn't loosen them so much that they came undone? Was it one or more?" Cliff asks.

"I don't know," Owen begins. "All I know was I was mad at them for having a great life and next thing I know; I'm loosening his bolts. Oh my God, what have I done?" Owen puts his hands on his head and lays down on the bed.

"Don't panic. At least not yet." Cliff responds. "I'll tell them you were with me. We played video games all night."

"Thanks," Owen responds. "I'll write this paper and get out of that club. I promise."

"Good," Cliff sits on his bed. "How did you bypass the security cameras?"

"I waited till the front guy went to the bathroom. He takes a shit every night at the same time," Owen responded.

"In my hoodie?" Cliff shakes his head.

Owen grabs the hoodie. "I'll get rid of this. I'm going to town and I'm going to run an errand. I have to see if Dawson is ok. I'll get rid of the hoodie." Owen explains as he gets up.

"I loved that hoodie," Cliff remarks. "Don't admit to the dad what you did. He'll take you down no matter how sorry you are.

Owen nods and leaves. He heads to the bus stop with the hoodie stuffed in his backpack.

He goes over and over in his head what he'll ask at the hospital and then how he'll tell Archie to forget everything. Maybe stay this weekend at the club and get all the info he needs and then leave forever. No problem.

The front doors of the hospital were already locked because visiting hours were already over. Owen headed to the Emergency entrance. He walked in and headed to the desk. The lady told him unless he was family, he couldn't visit. Suddenly, a disturbance outside the door caused everyone to look and Owen slipped through the door past staff.

He stood outside of Dawson's room and was now having second thoughts about everything he thought of on the way over.

"Are you here to visit my brother?" a voice behind him asked. Owen smelled a familiar scent as he turned around and came face to face with the girl in the hallway earlier. "I'm Iris. I'm Dawson's sister. And you are?" Iris asked.

"I'm Owen Riley. I have the same psych class as Dawson," Owen smiled. Iris smiled back. "How is he?" Owen asked.

"Well, he now knows that he's off the football team for this year and he'll have to try out again next year. But he's still in all his classes. He had all the work done." Owen nodded, knowing that it meant he bought all the work.

"Did he hit a deer or something?" Owen asked innocently.

"No," Iris began. "His tire came off. Then he lost control of the car and hit a tree. He was lucky because if that tree wasn't there; he would have gone over the cliff and been killed."

Owen swallowed hard. "I'm so sorry. I heard what happened and just wanted to stop by and see if he was ok."

"You're so sweet. Thank you. Come on in. Everyone's inside." Iris said and pushed Owen through the door.

Inside the room, Dawson was laying on his hospital bed in his private room. Surrounded by his grandparents and his mom. His father was on the phone looking out his window and several of the football players were also inside.

"Owen Riley?" Dawson asked.

"Hey, I heard what happened and just wanted to see if you were ok?" Owen said quietly.

"I'm fine. Thank you." Dawson said, still surprised.

"Who is this dear?" Mrs. Myer asked.

"Mom this is Owen Riley," Dawson responded. "He's in my psych class."

"Are you taking psychology as a class or major?" Mrs. Myer asked.

"Major," Owen replied.

The woman now impressed, had drowned out the football players with their excitement. "A future Doctor, Iris," The grandmother announced.

"Not if he doesn't pass this final paper," Carson sneered. All eyes returned to Owen.

"I'm good. Dr. Forsythe read my first pages and was impressed." Owen responded.

"Mine is already turned in," Carson grinned.

"Mine wasn't bought," Owen sneered back. Carson stood up along with the others just as a nurse walked in.

"Visiting hours are over. It's time for much-needed rest," she interrupted.

The mother felt the tension and stood up in front of Owen. "Boys time to go." She turned to Owen. "Thank you for stopping by and checking on my son."

Dawson looks at Carson and adds, "Iris, why don't you walk Owen to the door." Iris smiles at her brother and Owen is surprised by his response. "Owen, thanks for stopping by and checking on me."

Owen nods. "Get better, dude. Bye, Mr. and Mrs. Myer." The father nods and the mom smiles as do the grandparents.

Carson starts for the door but the grandmother gets up. "Carson, can you walk me to my car please?"

"What?" he turns and knows he's being stopped. "Yes, ma'am." Owen and Iris reach the front door. "I hit a nerve," Owen replies.

"Do you have a cell phone?" Iris asks.

Owen holds it up. She takes it and puts her number in it. "Call me sometime. We'll have lunch or something." He smiles and nods.

"Iris. Home." Mr. Myer snaps his fingers. She sighs and hands him back his phone. "You must focus on your studies dear," the grandfather responds to her as she walks over to her father.

"Yes, grandpa. I'm at a 3.4" Iris reminds him.

"But you could be at a 4.0" he responds back.

They leave and Owen sees the crew heading in his direction. Owen eyeballs the bus. He runs out the door, almost hitting a woman who is mopping the floor. He runs toward the bus and makes it in time. He looks over at the door as the crew hits the door. Carson points at him on the bus and begins to run but slips on the floor. They all fall over each other as the woman who mopped the floor turns around and Owen recognizes her from the sociopath club.

Claudia turns and looks at Owen and blows him a kiss. His mouth falls open as the bus moves away. Claudia who is wearing scrubs, walks off and toward the parking lot. Owen can't make out anything else and turns back around. "I thought she was a bartender," Owen tries to think. He laughs out loud and relaxes. He knows that inside, this wasn't over. Far from it. This was just the beginning.

CHAPTER 8
THE GAME OF CAT AND MOUSE

Owen got into his dorm through the back door. He asked several of the other people in the dorm if they had seen any of the football players. No one had so he went up to his room. Cliff was already in bed. He laid down in bed and decided not to go to any of his classes in the morning. He would just keep a low profile.

Next day, Cliff was already out the door when he got up. Owen looked at his phone and all his classes had been cancelled so he had a free day. He decided to stay in the dorm and play video games all day to keep to himself and think things out. Tomorrow, he would meet the club on a more intimate level.

He knew that Claudia saved him which meant one or two things. Either they were watching him or Claudia wasn't really a bartender and had only said that to keep her identity protected. He wasn't sure which thought was more scary. The fact that they may be lying to him or the fact that they were watching him. Either way, they saved him. If Carson had caught him, they would have beat him up.

He looked at his phone. A text message from Iris.

Sorry about my parents. They are very school-focused. They expect a lot from Dawson and I. They are on him to go against the doctors and play football. Coffee tomorrow?

Owen looked at his bank account. He sighed. He texted back.

Tomorrow is not good. How about Sunday?

He waited. Then, a smile came across his face.

Sunday sounds great. Late afternoon, ok? Around 3 pm by the library.

He replied yes back and looked around the room. He logged into his account on the school page. He had enough for coffee and dinner if they went to the Lair and got something. He would just make an excuse that he had lots of work to do and had to stay close to the dorm. Owen sighed. Who was he kidding? Iris was so out of his league.

Cliff texted him that he was out with his parents till Sunday to stay safe. He felt bad how things had gone between them. Owen smiled. Someone yelled mail was there so Owen ran downstairs. Once in a while he got lucky and today was that day. He had received a box from his parents.

He ran upstairs and opened it. Mom had made cookies and sent a blanket and a card. Everyone said hello and that they missed him. Mom said that Dad was slowly coming to terms with him being in college. His younger brother wanted to stay home and run the business which made him happy. His father even bragged that his son was going to be a Doctor someday. Owen smiled from ear to ear. Most importantly, inside the card were three crisp $100 bills. Owen sighed. Things were certainly turning up for him today. Maybe this was a sign.

Next morning, he stood in front of the red door. Owen had his notebook and pen in hand ready to do interviews. He knocked on the door and the slide came open. He smiled and the door opened.

"Owen welcome home," a man whom he had not met yet greeted him.

"Thank you. And you are?" Owen held out his hand.

"I'm Manford. I clean up around here. I was retired but everyone does something to keep the club going. So, I do that a few times a week." Manford replied. "You hungry?" he asked. "I'm making breakfast."

"No, I'm good. I had leftover pizza." Owen said, sighing. Manford saw his reaction and laughed.

"Ahh, the life of a college student. Hot pizza. Cold pizza." Manford laughed. Suddenly Manford looked behind him. "Did you hear that?"

Owen looked. "I didn't hear anything." Manford laughed and pointed to the counter.

"Sit right there, Owen. I'll fix you up some proper breakfast. Like your mama would make." he smiled.

Owen smiled and sat down. Soon, they ate eggs, bacon, toast and the most delicious potatoes Owen had ever had. The front door opened and Archie came in along with Wrangler, Rio and Baker. Manford gets uneasy and Owen notices that.

"Come along, Owen. We want to show you our world," Archie smiles and motions to the door.

Owen gets up and turns and thanks Manford who looks worried. "I'm going to keep him company," Baker pats Manford on the back. The door opens as Everett comes in and goes to the back. Owen says nothing and follows Archie out the door with Rio. Wrangler walks over to Manford and grins.

"Is everything ok?" Owen asks.

Archie motions to a car. He sees the paper and pen and takes it from Owen. He throws it into the garbage can. "No notes. Do everything in your head. It's cleaner that way. You don't leave behind…. mistakes."

Owen nods.

"It's ok to ask questions but wait till we are not in the open to ask them. Ask them when it's only us." Archie explains.

Owen starts to get that uneasy feeling you get when you try something new and unsure about it. Like going to that first scary movie as a kid by yourself. You want to but you know you shouldn't. But you do.

Owen got into the car. The driver was someone he had never seen before. "Owen, this is Banick, our driver." Archie explains. Banick said nothing but just nodded which is what Owen did also.

They drove for about 45 minutes and soon they were out in the middle of nowhere. They came across a piece of land where the driver stopped in front of a closed fence. Rio put on gloves, got out of the car and opened the gate as Banick drove them through onto the property; Rio then closed the gate and got back into the car.

No words were spoken on the drive there. Owen wanted to tell them what happened to Dawson but he had a feeling they already knew. They probably also knew about Iris and his feelings for her. Finally, they stopped at their destination.

They walked up to a cabin that didn't look like much. It was dusty and dirty. Archie raised his hand to Owen to be quiet. Owen nodded. Archie opened the door and looked around and finally hit a switch and waited. Rio stared at his watch. Then marked a down count with his hands from 5--4---3---2---1. He smiled.

"We're good." Archie said and the men came in. Owen was confused more than anything. They took Owen to the back door and out to the shed. "We're going there?" Owen asked. Archie smiled.

They walked to the shed and inside, they locked the door behind them. Inside the shed, they removed the floor. Under the floor was a handle and they opened it and Rio pulled out a flashlight dramatically that Owen thought was a gun. All three men laughed. Rio went downstairs and flipped a switch.

Archie motioned Owen and down they went. A long tunnel with motion lights led the way as the four of them walked the long walkway. Then they got to a door. Owen swallowed hard and Archie opened the door. The door led into a garage that was well-maintained.

The garage held five cars. They walked to the backdoor and into it led to a huge kitchen. They were obviously in a house. Archie led them to the living room and opened the shades. Outside showed a beautiful lake. Owen looked out the window at the view. "Wow what a view," he smiled. The men all smiled. Rio headed to the kitchen and Banick started toward the bar.

"This is where we do all our meetings and our decisions." Archie explained.

"I thought you did everything at the club?" Owen seemed perplexed.

"No, that's where we meet and greet. That's where we unwind. Socialize. But here is where we make all the decisions as an entity." Archie replied.

"Can I ask questions here?" Owen asked.

Archie nodded.

"Do you all meet together as a group?" Owen asked.

No one answered his questions but Archie. Owen noticed this. He was obviously in charge.

Archie responded to him. "Society has a set of rules to live by. So do we. Our club has rules. We meet here. The entity. We make decisions as an entity here. Then we carry them out."

"How many of the group are there?" Owen asked thinking of all the things he just said.

"There are exactly 22," Archie sat down and motioned Owen to sit down. "We are in charge. The number 22 represents the master builder where dreams evolve into reality. The number 22 is the sign of balance, rebirth, adaptability, ambitions, confidence, and discipline."

"So, you have 22 at all times?" Owen asks.

Archie smiles. "At the moment we have 24. Two must step aside or…." moves hand flat and away from his body. Owen knew this meant someone would be killed. Archie's phone goes off. He reads the text and clears it. He nods at Rio.

"Can you help me with something outside?" Rio asks. Banick nods and they leave.

"So, you said the word entity?" Owen looked confused.

Archie smiles. "How's your paper coming along?"

Owen rolled his eyes. "Well, I have the beginning and I just need examples and then wrap it up. The examples have to be pretty strong." Archie looks towards the window and guides Owen toward the kitchen as Rio shoots Banick in the head outside in front of the window with a silencer. Wrangler has now shown up and Rio and him toss the body over the edge into the water. The body floats away. Rio rakes the leaves while Wrangler takes the gun and silencer and puts them into a bag and drives away.

"Are you hungry, Owen?" Archie asks him.

"No, Manford made me breakfast," Owen replies. He turns suddenly and looks toward the window and then back again. "Archie isn't your real name, is it?"

Archie smiles. "No, it's not. It's my middle name. My real name is Granville Archie Montgomery. Archie kind of just stuck when I grew up. I was named after my grandfather. So, I only use it when I'm working. I'm in the Yellow Pages."

Owen nods. "Does everyone go by their middle name?"

"No just me," Archie grinned. "We're not ashamed of who we are. Society has pegged us as monsters. Most of us have high-power jobs. CEOs, lawyers, doctors. We started this club because others came forward or we ran into one another in our positions and we wanted to help them grow in mainstream society. It's you who are the outcasts, not us. We could survive and grow without you."

"So, what do you do here in this house?" Owen asks.

"We make decisions for all of us. If one of us has a problem with a coworker or a spouse, we help them with that problem. Help them work it out." Archie says proudly.

Owen thinks for a moment. "You helped me, didn't you?" Archie smiles. Owen continues. "You helped me with Dawson."

Archie nods. "You loosened the bolts on the car but not enough where anyone would have noticed or done anything. I had one of the club members loosen them a bit more." "We could have killed him," Owen says sternly.

"Watch the attitude," Rio arrives through the door and points at Owen who looks to the floor and back at Archie who watches him.

"We could have…I'm just saying," Owen says again.

"No. If we wanted to kill him, we would have cut his breaks," Archie begins and checks his watch. "Now, this will look like a school prank. They'll think it was an ex-girlfriend, or a rival from another school or even another member of his team."

"What if it comes back to me?" Owen asks.

"It won't," Rio sits between the two of them. Archie is sitting on the chair on the left of the room and Owen is on the chair on the right while Rio sits on the couch. "You unplugged the cameras and we took out the DVD that was recording. A blank one was put in its place. So, they have nothing."

"How long have you been watching me?" Owen asks.

"Since you've made contact and asked to interview us," Archie explains, always keeping his tone even when he speaks. "Do you have regret?"

Owen thinks a moment. "No," and shakes his head. "I'm still unsure, though."

Rio smiles. "That's expected. It's the unknown."

"So, what kind of problems do all of you fix for the club?" Owen asks.

Archie smiles and so does Rio. "This is where you will be able to write your paper. From the examples I am about to give to you. You'll have to only use first names." "I'll change the names," Owen reassures him.

"You don't have to," Rio tells him. "You can use our first names. We don't mind."

Owen surprised by this, sits back and nods. Archie loves his expression and laughs.

"Use my example first," Rio gets excited. Archie takes a drink and points at him as he holds his shot glass.

Archie begins.

> Rio works in a factory. He works Monday thru Friday from 8-5. Every day his boss would patrol the floor to make sure everything ran the way a factory should. Rio is a hard worker. Diligent. The foreman would walk through once a week with the owner to show each area's progress. The owner would arrive with his wife. The wife, always dressed nicely, was ignored by her husband. She had a bruise under her eye or held her arm close to her. She always looked toward the door as if she was trying to escape. The owner would have her walk behind and snap his fingers at her as if she was a dog. One day, he told her to wait in the cafeteria for him while he did his rounds. Rio left his area and got a coke. He saw her there looking out the window. She opened the window and looked down as if she was

deciding to jump. Rio put the can of coke by her arm which startled her and brought her back to reality. He talked to her calmly and told her she had a lot to live for. She thanked him for his kindness. He told her that not all guys are jerks and she could leave him. She told him she couldn't. It was complicated. Then, he arrived and she then had to leave. The line boss arrived and warned Rio to stay away from her. The owner would never let her go. He told Rio that she was brought over from another country and that he had bought her from her family and she was given a life of luxury in exchange for her freedom. Soon, the factory had problems and the owner had to come in several times a week, and each time he brought her and placed her in the cafeteria. Soon, Rio and her started passing notes. Rio learned she was 12 when she was brought over and that he had taken her virginity by force. She had several children, all taken from her except one boy. Rio wanted to marry her, find her children, return them to her and raise them as their own. So he came to us and we helped him. I was his lawyer and because of what he did, he went to jail for 20 years.

Because she was married to him, she got the factory. Wrangler helped with all the children. Everett arrested him and Francine was the judge.

Owen leaned back and smiled. Rio nodded. "I have five kids now and I am very happy. She is very happy."

"And you are very rich," Owen pointed at him.

"It was never about the money," Rio explained. "It was about love. And writing a wrong."

Owen nodded. "So, everyone in the group has a job?"

Archie shakes his head no. "Everyone is employed out in the real world but they bring their expertise to the club. Some we can use and some do other things for us. For example, Manford cleans and Banick drives, or at least he used to." Everyone chuckles.

"Manford looked a bit stressed when we left today," Owen remarked.

Archie and Rio exchange looks. "Manford is on probation from the club for talking," Archie explains.

"You have to be careful who you talk to about the club and what you say about us," Rio warns Owen.

"I will." Owen begins. "And remember, I'll let you read my paper before I turn it in."

"So, can I use Rio's story as an example of the club?" Owen asks.

Rio nods. Archie stands up. "They're ready for us," he replies toward Rio and motions Rio to the door. "Come, Owen we'll show you firsthand how we help each other. This way you'll be a part of the team and that will give you two things. One, another example for your paper and two, you'll show everyone that you're one of us."

Owen stops for a second and shakes his head slightly at the thought of Archie's comment. He wasn't one of them. He wasn't a sociopath. But then he thought of what Cliff said to be careful not to be drawn into their world. Then he thought of his paper. Him seeing the actual setup and carried-out antics of the club would make a great part of his paper. Plus, if he didn't like what they were doing, he would simply say no.

Archie sat in the back with Owen as Rio backed out and headed to the gate. "Where did the other driver go?" Owen asks.

Archie smiled and said nothing. "He wasn't feeling too well. He had a headache," Rio began and looked back at Archie who smirked. "I told him to lay down and I would do the driving today."

Owen nodded.

"Can you get the gate for us, Owen?" Archie asks. Owen nods and gets out of the car and opens the gate as Rio laughs and Archie smiles. The car goes through and Owen closes the gate. He heads to the car as Archie texts:

> Everything at the gate is set. Take care of the cabin. His glass Was the green one.

We see a message on his phone that reads: Read by 49 people. The men drive to the city but on the opposite side where Owen was not familiar with. They stop at a Safeway parking lot. Another car is next to them with several people inside. On the opposite side, another car drives up with people inside. All three cars roll down the windows.

"Who's the new guy?" a man in the one car asks.

"This is Owen, everyone," Archie explains.

The guy nods and so does everyone else. "Why are we here?" Owen whispers. Rio holds his finger to his mouth and points at Archie. Owen shuts up and looks at Archie who ignores the situation and continues.

"We all know why we're here. But I'll explain it for Owen here so he understands." Archie begins. "Our Claudia was attacked last night after work. She wants to handle things on her own but we won't let her. Anger gives way to mistakes as we all know. Control is everything. We must always have the upper hand. We must always take care of our own family. Whose turn is it to take the lead?"

"Mine!" the man in the right car sitting on the passenger side says excitedly. Everyone smiles or laughs at his excitement.

"Who's next?" Archie asks.

"We're tied," a man in the other car says, pointing at himself and the man next to him.

"You'll both share the 2nd spot and play it out. Don't get careless and don't get aggressive. Let it play out. Rhett, you play the customer." Archie points.

Rhett smiles. Owen had seen him at the club but the others he had not. Rhett was thin. He wore a suit the night before and was in a suit now again. The suit was perfectly pressed. His hair was slicked back and his voice and mannerism let Owen to believe he was gay.

"Everyone knows what they are supposed to do?" Archie asks. Everyone nods. Owen saw some were glaring at the building. "Let's do this for Claudia." Everyone repeated, "for Claudia." The doors opened and everyone got out. There were 11 of them in total. Two went to the back of the store. The others broke off in either pairs or singular going into the store, including Archie and Owen.

As they walked toward the store, Owen asked, "What should I be doing?"

They walked into the store and headed for the carts. The others could already be seen with carts or hand baskets or just walking.

"You should be helping me get what I need," Archie pushed a cart to Owen. "You push the cart. I'll shop."

They started down an aisle. Archie received a text. He reads it while Owen watches him and looks around the store, unsure of what they are doing.

"He's outside on break. So we need to slow down and take our time." Archie whispers.

Owen nods. He looks over as an elderly lady is trying to reach something on the top shelf. One of the men from another car comes around the aisle and helps her. She thanks him. He goes by not making any eye contact with Owen or Archie.

Archie's phone goes off again. "He's coming in now," Archie whispers. Both Owen and Archie see a man walk from the back where the product is stored to the inside of the store. He walks over to the produce and starts rearranging fruit.

A different man from one of the cars goes in the back where the product is held and comes out with a mop bucket and mop. He is wearing a Safeway smock. Owen can't believe how bold he is. Archie winks at Owen and they are closer by the produce but not in the area. Just where they can both observe.

Rhett walks into the area and pulls a cantaloupe out of the middle of the stack, causing the entire display to roll onto the ground.

"Oh my. How did this happen?" Rhett says loudly.

The man whom they targeted turns and runs over there and sees the mess. "Oh no, I just stacked those," he says.

"I'm so sorry," Rhett overdoes his voice. "Do you need help picking these balls up?"

The man sees that Rhett is gay and steps back, holding his hand up. "No thanks. I got it.

Just go."

Rhett smiles and grabs two cantaloupes and holds them up and says loudly, "Wow, these balls are huge. Are yours this big, honey?"

The man is getting very upset and walks to the front and gets a cart and returns. He starts slowly, putting the cantaloupe from the floor into the cart. He is getting very frustrated as Rhett is still there, remarking on sizes and shapes of the cantaloupe and making sexual innuendos to them. The man is about to explode when overhead the intercom comes on:

Ben, we need a mop to aisle 3 for cleanup. Ben aisle 3.

Rhett looks at his nametag which reads: Ben. He smiles and takes his cart passed Archie and Owen. Ben quickly picks up the remainder of the cantaloupe and pushes the cart into the back area and heads back with a mop and bucket. He puts up the signs "caution" in the area and mops up the spill.

One of the men is there and apologizes for the spill. "No problem, Sir," Ben tells him. Overhead, the intercom comes on:

Ben, we need a mop to aisle 5 for cleanup. Ben aisle 5.

Ben stands up in disbelief. "You've got to be kidding me." He says out loud. He walks away with his bucket to the next aisle spill. The guy in that aisle removes the caution signs and goes to the back and just sets them there. Ben mops up the area and a manager comes around the corner angrily.

"Ben!" he yells.

"Yes Sir, Mr. Thompson!" Ben answers.

"Ben, you know you are supposed to put out Caution signs on a spill," the manager yells for everyone to hear.

"Yes sir, Mr. Thompson. But we only had the one set and I used them on the other spill." Ben explains.

"No, you didn't because a man just fell in aisle 3," Mr. Thompson yells. "We have five sets of these things. Get back there and get them out NOW!"

Ben runs to aisle 3 and a man is on the floor complaining his knee hurts. Several people are helping him. Mr. Thompson is now there also asking what he can do. Ben runs to the back and in plain site are the caution signs. Ben looks around and can't believe they're there. He grabs two sets of them and puts them both up.

The man who fell is elderly and is the husband of the woman who couldn't reach the shelf item. She is very concerned. "I need an ambulance for my husband," she yells. Mr. Thompson sighs and calls for one right away.

"Don't you people put caution signs up when you mop?" the old man cries out. "My knee. My knee."

"Henry, don't move. An ambulance is coming. I'm calling our lawyer," she announces. Mr. Thompson glares at Ben and motions him to the front.

"Ben, help out with bagging," he yells. "I'm so very sorry, sir. Did anyone see him fall?"

"Are you saying my husband is faking this?" the woman yells.

"No. No. Of course not. This is our fault," Mr. Thompson admits. One man is videotaping while a woman tries to calm the wife.

"Sir, wait for the ambulance. You shouldn't move." One of the men from the car announces. "I saw him fall. It was horrible. There was no sign here warning of a spill."

Mr. Thompson sighs. Owen and Archie go into the line where Ben is bagging. Rhett asks if he can take cuts and Archie says, "Of course, sir. I have plenty of time. Go right ahead."

"Thank you. You're so kind." Rhett winks. The girl behind the counter is timid and is trying to ring everything up and Ben looks around to see if he can go elsewhere.

"Bill, trade places with me," Ben whispers but Bill shakes his head no.

"Going on break, dude. Sorry." Bill takes off his smock and heads out for a cigarette.

"You are so beautiful," Rhett tells the shy girl.

She thanks him and nervously moves her hair back. "Really, I love your hair and that cut looks so good. You know what would look better? These earrings." Rhett removes a pair from his pocket and hands them to her. "I want you to have these."

"I couldn't," she nervously looks around. "They're so beautiful. Are they handmade?" "Yes, a friend of mine makes them. Her name is Claudia," Rhett says and looks right at Ben. Ben steps back and stares at Rhett. He looks around and sees all the men suddenly stop and glare at him.

Ben nervously puts the food in the bag. He eyeballs Rhett who pushes the earrings into the cashier's hand. She puts them in her pocket and thanks him. Rhett pulls out all his coupons and takes his time going over them.

"Can we hustle here? We have a line," Ben yells.

"Rude!" Archie says loudly. Mr. Thompson comes around the corner.

"I'm sorry," Rhett says loudly. "I think Macy here is doing an amazing job and you should give her credit. I am very happy with her amazing service but you have been rude to me since I got here. Is it because I'm gay?"

Ben looks as everyone stops and looks at him. Mr. Thompson glares at Ben. "Thank you, Macy.

Can someone take my bags to my car?" Rhett asks. Mr. Thompson folds his arms.

"Ben would love to help you, sir!" Macy winks at Rhett who smiles.

"Thank you!" Rhett sashays away and whispers to Ben, "I don't want to break a nail."

Mr. Thompson walks to the window and watches as Ben walks with Rhett to the car. "Who are you?" Ben asks Rhett. "Really, who are you?" Rhett smiles.

"Your nightmare comes to life asshole," Rhett looks over at the window and waves. Mr. Thompson looks and then sees the ambulance and turns back to the elderly couple. As the couple is tended to, a huge truck parks in front of the window. It's a moving truck and blocks the view. He is trying to get into the road to make a right turn and is waiting his turn.

Owen looks at Archie who smiles. "All according to plan," he whispers. They leave and head to the door. The truck leaves as the elderly couple is loaded into the ambulance.

"Oh my goodness," Archie says loudly. Mr. Thompson gasps. He runs out to the parking lot and pulls Ben off of Rhett.

"He hit me because I'm gay. He called me faggot." Rhett musters tears. A handful of people run to him to help him. Two men help Mr. Thompson with Ben.

"Have you lost your mind?" Mr. Thompson screams. "First the caution signs then this?"

Ben looks around. "They're all in this together. Don't you see?"

"What I see is an unemployed worker," Mr. Thompson yells. "You're fired, Ben."

Archie looks at Owen and raises his eyebrows a few times and then winks at the ambulance driver. Owen turns as the elderly couple waves at Owen. Owen turns in disbelief and sees a police car drive up.

Everett gets out of the car very seriously. "What's going on here?"

Everyone talks at once as another police car drives up. Mr. Thompson tells Everett what he knows and Everett looks at Rhett and offers a ride to the hospital or an ambulance to be called.

"I'm pressing charges officer," Rhett cries.

"Officer listen, this is all a scam. I've never seen these people before. This is all because I hit some girl the other day. It was at a bar called Moonshine and I hit her and these are her friends or something getting back at me," Ben admits.

"So you beat up a woman?" Everett asks him. Mr. Thompson shakes his head. Macy wipes Rhett's face with a tissue.

"You asshole," Macy announces. "I have to go back in. I'm so sorry this happened to you."

"Thank you honey," Rhett smiles. "It's part of gay life."

"Not in this city," Everett announces sternly. "We take gay bashing very seriously."

"Gay bashing?" Ben yells. "No! No!" Ben shakes his head. "This is all fixed."

"So, you're saying," Rhett starts. "That me as a gay man, goes to Moonshine, which is a known redneck bar, to be with someone named Claudia, whom I've never met and came here to out you, whom I've never seen before today so I can get beat up for being a gay man?"

The other officer comes back to Everett. "I just called Moonshine and they said they do have a bartender named Claudia who was attacked while walking to her car after work the other day. She was beaten up pretty bad. The guy tried to rape her and she fought him off but he beat her up. She was released this morning."

Everett arrests Ben and puts him in the back of the police car. Ben looks over at Rhett who winks at him. Rhett is helped into the back of the ambulance. The older lady and man wave at Ben. Ben looks at Archie who smiles. He looks at his coworkers who look at him with disgust and then at the witnesses, most who are from the car.

Everett drives away with Ben. "I bet you didn't think this day would go like this when you got up this morning, did you?" Everett asks him.

"No, I didn't," Ben says quietly.

"Well, it's going to get a lot worse for you boy," Everett glares at him. Ben sees his eyes and gets worried.

Archie walks over to his car and Owen gets inside. Once inside, Owen just shakes his head.

Archie looks at him and smiles. "You disapprove?"

"No, actually I think he had it coming. He was a jerk," Owen says. "Karma."

Owen looks at Archie. "That was well organized."

They take off and Owen looks at the police car and ambulance way ahead. "We're all those people involved?"

Archie replied. "Not all of them. Sometimes, we get lucky and everything just plays out perfectly. Like today. Some days, we have to improvise."

Owen laughs. "Now what?"

Archie looks out the window. "Now the Murphy's get a check from Safeway for pain and suffering and they go on that cruise they always wanted to go on."

Owen looks at him. "If he needs surgery on that knee."

Archie smiles. "He does need surgery but his insurance didn't cover all of it but Safeway will."

Owen watches as the cop car goes in the opposite way of the station. "But Rhett got beat up pretty bad."

Archie nods. "Yes, he did. He's into that. He likes getting hit. For him, it's sexual. He is also gay. So, the city will put Ben away for a hate crime. He won't go to jail for what he did to Claudia but he'll go away for what he did to Rhett. He's an angry young man full of issues and we'll take care of one of them. Rhett gets off and he'll get a big check from Safeway also."

Owen looks at Archie. "Are you going to be their attorney?" Archie nods. Owen continues. "Then Francine will get the case and Ben will go away and lose everything and Claudia will get justice."

Archie nods in agreement. "Now you know how our world works for us."

Owen nods and watches the police car head toward the river. "I'm starting to see how the club thinks."

Archie pats him on the back. Rio smiles and continues to drive.

CHAPTER 9
A DATE WITH DESTINY

Owen got out of the car in front of the walkway to school. He still had to walk across campus. He didn't mind the guys letting him out here because he had to digest all he learned and saw today. He wanted to distance himself also.

"Sorry we didn't drive you all the way to the other side but we figured this would be closer for you to have coffee with your new friend," Archie said as the car started off. Owen turned quickly. "What?" he yelled.

"Say hello to Iris for us, Owen. We'll text you soon," Archie yelled. Rio hit the horn twice and they were gone. Owen stepped back a few steps, shocked that they even knew about her.

Owen checked himself. He pulled out his cell phone and checked it. How did they know? Was his room bugged? His phone? The computer? Maybe one of his teachers was in the club. He ran his fingers through his hair.

"Boo!" Iris grabbed him from behind and he turned quickly, shocked. "I'm so sorry. Are you ok?"

"Yeah." Owen shook it off. "You just scared me, that's all."

"I'm so ready for some coffee!" Iris smiled and off they went. Owen looked back one time and then put his hand out and Iris took it. They walked hand in hand to the coffee shop.

They talked about likes and dislikes. They talked about their favorite movies and dreams. Places they both wanted to visit someday or places they've been. Iris loved to take pictures and she loved German food. Her favorite color was Blue and she had a puppy named Garfield. She loved tulips, standing in the rain, the Beatles, horses, and helping the poor. She wanted to marry and move far away from her parents and have two kids and adopt one.

Owen smiled. "I'm ok with all that."

She laughed. She learned a lot about Owen. His middle name was Lewis. He wanted to see the world and have a retirement home by the ocean so he could write. He wanted to name his first kid after his father and grandfather: Miles. He loved ice cream and video games. He had a dog named Hunter and a cat named Eevee, after his favorite Pokemon character.

"Do you want to go to a movie sometime?" Owen asked her.

"That would be nice," Iris said shyly.

"I mean, I don't have a car so we'd have to take the bus," Owen said, a little embarrassed.

"I would love that," Iris said sincerely. "I have a car but I'd really like to try the bus." "You've never been on a bus, have you?" Owen asked as they headed to the door.

"No," Iris said, laughing. "But I would love to try public transportation." They both cracked up laughing. Iris's phone rang and she looked at it and stopped laughing.

"Hi mom." Iris began. She walked away for a moment and Owen gave her the space she needed. She came back and grabbed his arm. "Would you like to have dinner at my parents' house tonight with me?"

"Wow, meeting the parents on the first get-together." Owen joked.

"Pleaseeeeeee," she whined. "Don't make me go there alone. I can drive you back home."

"Sure. Let me change." Owen asked, looking down at what he was wearing.

"No, you look fine. Let's go. The faster we go there, the faster we can leave," Iris explained.

"Wait, what? Are they that bad?" Owen asked seriously.

Iris smiled and nodded. "Yes, they are." and they ran off laughing.

The car stopped in front of a huge house. "Wow," Owen said, looking out the dash of the car. "This is like…ten of our houses."

"Yeah, my parents have to have the biggest and best of everything," Iris remarked, unimpressed with her family's home.

Owen understood. In his small town, their family had more than most. Maybe not the biggest house but a new car and newer clothes. Most of his classmates' families worked in the lumber yards and had hand-me-downs. So, Owen understood.

"They know I'm coming, right?" Owen asked as he shut the car door.

"Come on!" Iris said, ignoring the question.

"Oh man," Owen said out loud. He sighed and ran after her. They got to the front door at the same time. Iris knocked and then opened the door and went in.

"Miss Iris," a black woman came to greet her.

"This is Silvia, our maid and, at one time, my nanny," Iris hugged her.

"You hush girl before we both get into trouble," Silvia giggles. She was a large woman with a beautiful, broad smile. Her eyes glistened and Owen liked her instantly. He felt comfortable and accepted by her immediately.

"Where are they?" Iris whispered.

"In the den," Silvia hit her arm. "Who is this young man?"

"Silvia," Iris said proudly, "I'd like you to meet Owen Lewis Riley, the future Doctor of Psychiatry." Owen laughed. He held out his hand which impressed both ladies.

"Nice to meet you, Silvia," Owen said.

"Nice to meet you Mr. Riley," Silvia said, guiding the two to the den.

"You can call me Owen," Owen suggested. By their expression, he knew he had said something stupid.

The den door opened and Iris and Owen made their grand entry. Silvia grabbed Owen's arm and whispered to him. "Don't you listen to anything Mr. Meyer says. You're a good man. I can tell."

Owen didn't know what she meant but by the way Iris acted and the way Silvia acted, he was sure he was going to find out.

"Who is this Iris?" Mrs. Meyer asked. Mr. Meyer was pouring himself a drink. He looked over and looked Owen up and down. Mrs. Meyer slid her hand up and down Owen's arm which made him nervous. Everyone in the room noticed what she had done.

"Mother, this is Owen Riley; he goes to school with me at the university. You met him at the hospital when he came in and checked on Dawson." Iris reminded her.

"Oh yes, I remember," Mrs. Meyer smiled. She looked a bit drunk and was holding a glass of something.

"You're being a lush, Donna," Mr. Meyer announces. Mrs. Meyer rolls her eyes and sits down.

"So, I take it you're staying for dinner Mr. Riley?" Mr. Meyer asks.

"That's ok, isn't it Daddy?" Iris defends Owen.

"I hope it isn't an imposition, sir." Owen tries to be polite. Mr. Meyer sees through him and scoffs and walks into the dining room. Mrs. Meyer grabs a hold of his other arm and whispers to him.

"It's never an imposition. You're just being polite. He can be such a drag at times. Can't he, Iris?" Mrs. Meyer laughs.

Iris guides Owen next to her at the table. They all sit down, letting the ladies sit first. Mr. Meyer watches every move Owen makes. Several people bring food out and set it in front of everyone.

Owen smiles at each one of them and they smile back. Owen knows they're checking him out. Iris smiles. Mrs. Meyer asks for another drink and Mr. Meyer reminds her the time of the day and that she's had enough.

"Oh darling, you can never have enough of a good thing," Mrs. Meyer coos.

Unimpressed, Mr. Meyer directs his attention to Owen. Owen eyeballs all the silverware, unsure of which to use. Iris lifts her fork up and begins to talk to her father. Owen imitates her, hoping not to be ousted but both Mr. and Mrs. Meyer knew he doesn't know which one to use.

"How is the stock market today, Daddy?" Iris detours his attention.

"Average love," Mr. Meyer replies. "So, what do your parents do for a living, Owen?"

Iris hits her fork on the plate, making a loud noise. Her father knows what she's doing as does Owen. He looks at Silvia. He looks at Mr. Meyers and says "Mr. Meyers, I'm proud to say my parents opened up their own store in a small town. Raised five kids on their income and I got a scholarship to come to this university. My father was disappointed that I wanted to go to college. He wanted me to run the business. But I have bigger dreams. I want to be a Doctor. Maybe not the type of Doctor you're impressed by. The ones who save lives. I want to be a Doctor who saves minds."

Mrs. Meyers smiles and toasts Mr. Meyers with her glass. Mr. Meyers nods and Silvia winks at Iris. Irish grabs a hold of Owen's hand tightly. He knows he has won the table.

"Sounds like a great plan, Owen. Good job!" Mr. Meyer announces and Owen smiles.

"How is your son doing?" Owen changes the subject.

"He's fine. He'll be released tomorrow morning. That reminds me, Donna we need to go through his bathroom to make sure he won't fall. Remove the rugs in the hallway and upstairs," Mr. Meyer tells her.

Mrs. Meyer nods to Silvia who immediately goes and does the things Mr. Meyer had just asked his wife to do.

"I do believe his car was tampered with, though," Mr. Meyer tells them as he cuts his meat.

"What Daddy?" Iris is surprised. "Why would you think that?"

"Well, for one, all his bolts on his car tire were loosened on two wheels," Mr. Meyers begins. "That would be accidental if it had been one bolt on one wheel but all of them on two wheels? That's tampered with."

"Is security checking it out, dear?" Mrs. Meyers asked, concerned.

"To hell with them. I went to the police chief. He has detectives looking into it," Mr. Meyer raises his voice.

"Detectives Daddy?" Iris asks

"Yes, it's attempted murder," he responds. Owen stops eating and looks at Mr. Meyers who looks at him and points at his plate. "How's your steak son?"

"Fine Sir," Owen responds. "What did they find out?"

Mr. Meyer shrugs. "I talked to them about an hour ago. They talked with his teammates and all of them checked out. It wasn't the other team. They were out of town at a meet and were all accounted for. They checked his dorm and the security camera checked out and everyone was accounted for. That left the dorm where he was parked at. That dorm's security camera had been turned off. A blank DVD was found in the system. So someone either switched DVDs or they never turned the damn thing on."

Owen swallowed hard.

"What dorm do you belong to, Owen?" Mr. Meyer asks, popping a piece of steak into his mouth.

"Daddy!" Iris said excitedly. "You're not seriously thinking Owen had anything to do with this, are you?"

"I didn't know which dorm he was in," Mr. Meyer said in defense.

Owen held his hands up. "It's ok. It's ok. What do the police think will be their next move?" he asked.

"Well, they said they will now interview every person in that dorm and check for prints," Mr. Meyer explained.

Mrs. Meyer, bored with the conversation, changed gears and started a new conversation. She didn't like knowing that someone was crazy enough to try and kill her son. The rest of the evening was spent checking the house layout and looking at Mr. Meyer's collection of trophies and cars.

Iris announced they would be leaving and heading back to the university and Owen thanked them for a lovely evening and a delicious meal. He held out his hand to Mr. Meyer.

"Thank you, sir. I was also wondering if I may ask your permission to take your daughter out for a dinner and a movie, sir?" Owen gave direct eye contact.

Iris smiled at the chivalry he displayed. Mrs. Meyer smiled and nodded at Mr. Meyer who was not even impressed. "Yes, you may," he said coldly. Iris saw that and pulled Owen away. Owen didn't care. He was happy with that response.

On the way back, Owen and Iris giggled and talked about future classes, plans, and days off. Owen decided to kiss her on the cheek but when they went on their first date, he would make the big move.

"I thought he was quite a gentleman," Mrs. Meyers said as she headed upstairs. "Coming, dear?"

"I'll be right there love," he told her and headed to his den. He picked up the phone and made a call. "Jonathan, I need you to check out

Owen Riley for me. He's at the university in Sumner Hall and he's in the psychiatric program."

"You think he had anything to do with the car?" Jonathan asks.

"I don't know. But he knows my son. He's now trying to date my daughter. Something is just off on this kid. Check him out." Mr. Meyer ends the call.

He turns off the light and heads to bed.

Owen kissed Iris on the cheek and headed back to the dorm. Suddenly, he felt something coming up on him. He turned just in time to see Carson tackling him. Both fell to the ground.

Sawyer, Lincoln, Aldridge and some other team members followed. "Pick him up," Carson yelled and they did. "You think you're smarter than us? You think you can move in on my girl?" Carson punched Owen in the stomach as Sawyer and Lincoln held him by both arms.

"You don't own anyone. She's her own person," Owen could barely breath.

"Go to hell," Carson yelled and punched him in the face.

"Carson, stop!" a girl yelled from the dorm he just left. Carson turns and the others let go of Owen and he falls to the ground.

"Owen?" Cliff yells as he and several of the other guys from their dorm run over. "Are you ok?"

"You guys saw nothing, hear me?" Sawyer directs them. Several of them cower but the girl and Cliff do not.

"Shut up, Football nerd," Cliff bravely says. "Leave our friend alone."

"Yeah, go throw a ball or something," another said, trying to be cool.

The girl rolled her eyes and pointed into Carson's chest. "Do you want Iris to know you're doing this?"

"No," Carson admitted and walked away. He turns suddenly and says to Owen, "Stay away from her."

"I won't," Owen announces loudly. The girl smiles at him and the footballers come toward him.

"Come on, guys. Let's go. Leave the nerds to their video games." Carson laughs and they start to leave.

One of the guys from the dorm got the last word in. "Well, we may be nerds but when you're in the hospital on your 5th surgery and you get dropped from the team, we'll be marrying your ex-wife and living in our million-dollar mansions." Everyone laughed.

"Loser," Aldridge yelled.

"Poser," the same guy yelled. The guys laughed and helped Cliff take Owen back to the dorm.

Inside the dorm room, Cliff waited for them to be alone. Before he could say anything, Owen told him all about his day and everything he saw happen. Cliff then told him the police had come by and he had told them they spent the day watching Harry Potter series and playing video games. They went over their stories several times to make sure everyone was on the same page. The same games. The same movie and the same episode.

Owen sat down and wrote out his paper. He then printed it and went to bed. He was excited to see what Dr. Forsythe would say.

CHAPTER 10
A SHOT IN THE DARK

Dr. Forsythe read the paper in front of him. He looked up at Owen several times. He took off his glasses and then reapplied them. When he was done, he sat the paper down and leaned back in his chair.

"This is without a doubt the best paper in the class and in my entire career," Dr. Forsythe announced to Owen. Owen stepped back.

"Thank you, sir," he stammered.

"What happened to your eye?" Dr. Forsythe pointed.

"Football players," he responded.

"Idiots," Dr. Forsythe laughed. "Sit down. Sit down. Tell me what it was like? Tell me, will you go again? You must be careful. "

"I am being careful," Owen replied coldly.

Dr. Forsythe sighed and watched Owen as he nervously looked around. "You're getting paranoid. You're restless and short. This is not you, Owen."

Owen smiled. "Dr. Forsythe, you see me one time a day, five times a week along with hundreds of others. How in the hell…." Owen stops and straightens up in his chair.

"I see you, Owen." Dr. Forsythe begins. He walks over to him and sits next to him. "I see you. Look, we have these papers and all you have to do is to meet the criteria of the board, the university and the doctrine sets-up. It does not make you a doctor. Anyone can do this. How you react and respond to situations. How you help people reach their full potential …THAT is what makes you a doctor. You have that in you. Finish this paper. You have enough information."

"I didn't tell you everything," Owen explained. Dr. Forsythe leaned back in the chair.

"They have a second club house by a lake. They call themselves the entity and they have 22 people there who make decisions. However, I believe there are far more than 22 of them."

Dr. Forsythe gets up and removes his glasses and scratches his head. He leans on his desk. "Can you introduce me to them?" He asks.

Owen was suprised by this turnaround. "No. I can't. I'm not even supposed to be talking to you even though I'm sure they know I am. They know I have to show you my paper.

But I'm supposed to let them read it first."

"Would you be willing to wear a wire?" Dr. Forsythe asked.

Owen stands up. "Hell no!" He shakes his head several times and looks around. "Why would you even suggest that?"

"Owen, sit down," Dr. Forsythe begins. "I need you to calm down and hear me out." Owen sits down and crosses his arms.

"Go on," Owen says. "I'm all ears."

Dr. Forsythe rocks back and clears his throat. "Owen, I've heard rumors of this club. I brushed them aside. You are the first student I assigned this topic too that brought back actual examples of the existence of said club."

"Is this the first class you've assigned this to?" Owen asked, curious.

"No," Dr. Forsythe shakes his head. "This is the third class I've assigned it to."

"What did the other students bring back?" Owen asks.

Dr. Forsythe sighs. "Each class I assigned this topic to, I gave a total of 6 students this topic. Two in each class."

"What did they bring back, Dr. Forsythe?" Owen asked again.

Dr. Forsythe lowers his head and looks at Owen. "In the first class, both students disappeared and were never found." Owen's mouth falls open. Dr. Forsythe continues. "In the second class, one left the program and the other committed suicide."

Owen stands up. "So, you gave it to me? Was it random or did you choose me? Who was the other student who got this assignment?"

Dr. Forsythe walks over to Owen to put his arm on his shoulder but Owen pulls away. "Who Dr. Forsythe? Who was the other student?"

"Dawson Myer," Dr. Forsythe whispers. Owen steps back and grabs his book bag and starts to the door. He stops suddenly and turns and looks at Dr. Forsythe who is watching him. Owen goes back to Dr. Forsythe's desk and grabs his paper and puts it in his bag.

"We're not your psychiatric experiment. We're students. You're supposed to teach us. Not use as your psychological rats." Owen stammers.

"Owen, wait!" Dr. Forsythe yells. "Please." Owen stops and turns.

"Please don't judge me so harshly." Dr. Forsythe begins. Owen, unsure of how to respond, waits. "Can you introduce me to the club?" he asks, smiling.

Owen shakes his head. "Unbelievable. Dr. Forsythe, I won't have to." Owen starts to turn. "I think they already know."

Owen walks out of the classroom, leaving a stunned Dr. Forsythe. Owen walks into the library and sits in his usual spot. He runs his fingers through his hair which he always did when he was nervous.

He started to think he was a mouse in a room and in front of each door was a trap. In front of one door stood the sociopath club and in front of the other door stood Dr. Forsythe. Either exit, he'd be trapped. There was no other door. Owen looked to his right out the window and smiled. "No door," he thought, "but I can crawl out a window."

"Hey," a familiar voice said next to him. Startled Owen turns and is faced with Dawson and his crew. "We need to talk."

Owen wasn't sure if they were there to beat him up or what their plan was. Owen stood up. "How…how are you feeling?" he asked.

Dawson put his hand up. "Don't pretend you care. Let's talk, you and I…. alone in the bathroom." He motions to the bathroom. Owen eyeballs the others who start to follow. "You guys…. wait here. I got this. Just give us a minute. Watch the door."

"You got it, buddy," Carson glares at Owen.

The two go into the bathroom. They wait for another student to finish. He comes out of the stall and senses the intensity of the two. He washes his hands and then wipes them on his pants and leaves right away.

"So, what's up?" Owen begins but Dawson steps to him face to face which cuts him off abruptly.

"I know you messed with my car. I know you like my sister." Dawson begins.

"What makes you think I would do something like this?" Owen looks away.

"It's all over your face. Plus, you were seen by a couple who were making out in their car," Dawson added.

"I loosened the nuts a bit," Owen said honestly. "I only did one wheel."

"I know," Dawson began. Owen was surprised. "They also saw another guy loosen them more and then another tire. So, you didn't cause the accident. The other person did." "Dude, I'm so very sorry. I don't know what I was thinking. Do you know who might have done it?" Owen asked.

"You and I both know it was the sociopath club," Dawson says bluntly. Owen looks up and they make eye contact.

Owen whispers. "You know about them?"

"I made contact for my paper. Earl told me about them and then went missing. So, I looked at his notes. His roommate let me eyeball his computer. I put the dots together. I made contact and asked them if they knew where he was. They said, at their suggestion he left and went to another school. He's at Arizona state now. He's majoring in something else. He's ok." Dawson turned to the mirror and started messing with his hair.

"Wow," Owen turned and looked at the mirror. He placed both hands on the sink. "You know Dr. Forsythe set us up. He knew about all this. He put this paper out two years ago and two sets of students got the same assignment as us. Two disappeared, one left the program and one committed suicide."

Dawson looked at Owen from the mirror and shook his head. "Unbelievable," Dawson replied.

"I know. I don't know what to do?" Owen said quietly.

"You have enough for your paper. Just leave. Stop contact. Hand your paper in. Forsythe will give you an "A" just because you know. You're golden. Then next semester, you'll have a new teacher. My dad will take care of that when I tell him what all happened." Dawson explains.

"You ok Dude?" Lincoln asks, opening the door.

"Yeah, just a few more minutes to wrap it up," Dawson waves him on. The door shuts.

"You're going to tell your Dad?' Owen asks.

"Just what needs to be told," Dawson tells him. "That I got a paper assignment and our professor set the class up and I was his pawn. That I could have died. He'll lose his job and his tenure."

"I like your sister," Owen blunts out, trying to change gears in the conversation.

"I know. She likes you too." Dawson leans his back against the sink, looking away from the mirror with his arms folded. "You make her happy. It's the first time I've seen her laughing and smiling in a long time."

"So…" Owen asks. "What do you want me to do?"

Dawson looks at him. "I think you're innocent in all this. I think you wanted to impress Dr. Forsythe with a good grade and you needed this to pass. I think you got caught up in this and unlike many of us here, we can pay for papers, not that is fair or right or whatever. The point is I don't blame you. I could tell you were sorry in the hospital when you came. You make my sister very happy. Don't hurt her. She matters to me."

"Got it." Owen sighed. "What about your Dad?"

Dawson grinned and started to the door, slapping Owen's shoulder. "That is your punishment. He'll figure it out that you were the other student. You'll have to deal with his wrath."

Owen sighs and looks at the floor as Dawson leaves. Owen sighs. One of his doors suddenly had a crack. Dawson's father would have Dr. Forsythe fired by the end of the quarter. He had the "A" in the bag. The only obstacle now was to back out of the club.

Owen left the bathroom and headed to the dorm. He stopped in the lobby to check for mail. Nothing today. He wished mom had sent more snacks. He loved and missed her home-baked goods. Today would be a great day just to work at the store. Maybe coming to university was not a good fit for him.

The TV was on in the lobby and as Owen turned, the news was on. He listened in as he waited for the elevator.

The body was that of what appears to be a 34-year-old male. Medium height with dark hair. He was wearing a checkered shirt with tie and black jeans. Again, a man was found floating in the East River early this morning with a single gunshot wound to the head. No ID was found with the body. If you have any information on this case or the other body police found, please contact them.

"You need the elevator, dude?" a student asked. Owen didn't give eye contact and just shook his head no.

"Shame on all those bodies they keep finding," a man's voice said next to Owen. Owen turned and came face to face with Wrangler.

"Bodies?" Owen whispered.

"Yeah, the one they found in the alley last night. Black man. I think his name was Manford or Mumford or something." Wrangler grins as he popped gum in his mouth.

"Can I help you, sir?" the student behind the counter asks.

"Um yeah, I'm looking for my nephew. I don't think he's in this building. I'll try the next one. My bad." Wrangler smiles.

"I could look him up for you if you'd like," the student offers, going to the computer.

Wrangler looks at him and thinks. His phone beeps. He looks down and at the student. "Never mind. He just texted me. He's in the library. Sitting on the second level, right by the bathroom. I guess it's his favorite spot." Wrangler waves at the student who nods. Wrangler goes to the door and looks at Owen. "Have a good day."

Owen looks at the TV and recognizes the clothes as Banicks and he knows the door he needed to get out of just locked forever. Owen needed help. But he didn't know who he could turn too.

CHAPTER 11
SETTING UP FOR JENGA

Owen laid on his bed and stared at the ceiling, trying to figure out every scenario he could to fix this. Cliff walked in and threw his book bag on the chair. Cliff began talking about how crappy his day had been while he made something to eat. He looked over at Owen.

"You ok, dude?" Cliff asks. Owen looks at him with tears in his eyes. "Oh my God, what happened?" Cliff asks, sitting next to him. He hands him his meal. "I made this for you."

Owen laughs and collects himself. He tells Cliff everything. Cliff leans back and is blown away. "You have to go to the president of the University and tell them everything. Then the police."

"They know everything before it happens. Or they're making it happen. It's like I'm playing a game of Jenga and I'm watching from over there," Owen points to the door. "And I know that the pieces are going to eventually fall and I'm watching them fall in slow motion and I can see every move but the one I'm supposed to make."

"Dude, that's deep," Cliff replies. "Ok, we don't know for sure that one body is the one guy and lots of guys wear plaid shirts and pants."

"Not jeans and a tie and the same fricking jewelry." Owen reminds him.

"Ok, so that guy was killed. Ok. You didn't see anything or hear anything, right?" Cliff asks.

Owen nods. "And how many people do you know named Manfred?" Owen stammers.

"Ok, now I'm getting nervous. Would they come here? Do they know I'm your roommate? Your friend?" Cliff asks.

"I saw one in the lobby pretending to look for someone. I think it was to show me they're in control. It's a mind game for sociopaths. It's how they roll. They stay in control and make you feel that you did something wrong." Owen explains.

The phone suddenly rings and they both look at it. Cliff answers it. "Hello?" "Hello?" He hangs up. "No one was there." Both boys look at each other and back at the phone. Owen looks out the window and sees only students. He looks around the room. Cliff helps him. They find nothing. Owen motions him and they go into the bathroom.

"Our room is bugged," Owen says.

"It was a coincidence. That's all. Dude, you're getting paranoid. That's what they want." Cliff tells him.

"Do you know anyone who can figure out if a room is bugged? Or have cameras hidden?" Owen asks desperately.

Cliff sees this is important to him. "Dude, we live in a dorm full of comic book geeks, computer nerds, and Trekkies. I got this. Take a shower and a nap and we'll go out for dinner. My treat."

Owen nods and grabs his towel. Two hours later, the guys were sitting in front of the buffet.

"Hey there! Fancy meeting you here!" Iris said, sitting down. "Hi, I'm Iris." she holds her hand out to Cliff who shakes it.

"Hi, I'm shocked. Actually, I'm Cliff. I'm just shocked you're with him." Cliff says jokingly. Everyone laughs.

"Well, I'm done so I think I'll go back to the dorm and play some videogames and cram for my final. You, ok?" Cliff asks Owen. Owen nods.

"Nice to meet you," Iris tells him.

"Nice to meet you, Iris," Cliff winks at Owen and holds a thumbs up. Iris and Owen laugh.

"I'm glad you're here. I need to talk to you." Owen tells her.

"I need to talk to you also," Iris tells Owen.

Owen thinks to himself. Tell him what? Oh no, did Dawson tell her about their conversation? He looked at her as she waited. "Lady's first," Owen blurts out.

"Ok," Iris says as she leans back in her chair. "Here we go. I like you, Owen. I like you a lot. You make me feel like I can just be myself. I don't have to pretend around you. I am heading up to the ski lodge this weekend coming and would really love for you to come with me."

Owen sighed and leaned back. He smiled and said, "I would love to. Will your parents be joining us?"

"No," Iris smiled and got up. "Just you and me. A fireplace. A Jacuzzi. And the weekend."

Owen smiled, knowing what she was getting at. "Awesome," he said like a teenager and felt embarrassed. Iris smiled and skipped away like a teenager.

"I'll pick you up Saturday morning so be ready. See you at your dorm," she yelled as she left.

Owen smiled and headed to the dessert table. He looked at himself in the mirror of the buffet glass and touched his face. "I need to clean up better."

Iris got to her dorm and walked in to be faced by her father. "Where were you?" he asked, looking around her room.

"How did you get in here, Daddy? How long have you been here?" Iris asks angrily. "Why are you so defensive?' Mr. Meyer asks.

"I'm not. I'm sorry." Iris deflates immediately. "I'm just tired. Finals are coming."

"Next week, right?" Mr. Meyer asks.

"Yes," Iris sits on her bed. "I was eating dinner and now I'm going to study."

"Your mother tells me you're heading to the ski lodge this weekend. Is that wise before finals?" Mr. Meyer asks, prying.

"Daddy, in university finals are on different days for most students. This weekend will be loud and full of parties. I need to study so I'm going to the ski lodge to unwind, relax and study." Iris tells him.

He nods. "No, boy's right?" he asks.

She looks away and back. "I'm bringing a boy, yes."

"Carson?" Mr. Meyer asks.

"No, Daddy. I'm not dating Carson. I've never been interested in Carson, Daddy." Iris tells him.

"He's interested in you." Mr. Meyer tells her.

"Daddy, he's a jock. I don't like jocks. I like men who can think for themselves. Like you Daddy," Iris stands up to face him.

He rolls his eyes. "If I hadn't busted my knee and shoulder in High School. I would have been a jock," he tells her.

"I know Daddy. I know. But look at all that you have accomplished." Iris reminds him. "As long as it's not that Owen kid you're taking," Mr. Meyer says, surveying the room more.

"What's wrong with Owen?" Iris says angrily. Mr. Meyers looks at her but she doesn't back down. "I like Owen, Daddy. I like Owen a lot. He is the guy I'm taking to the ski lodge." Iris turns and lays on her bed, grabbing a book.

"No, you're not. Do you understand? I'm putting my foot down. You take him and I will pull you out of this university and send you to another one. I'll close your accounts. Take the car. No lodge. No vacation with your mom and I to Europe this year. Do you understand?" Mr. Meyer stands firm.

She looks at him. Iris gets up and faces her father and sighs. "I understand Daddy," Iris says sadly.

"Good girl. Your mom and I are going to spend the weekend at the Johnson's Lakehouse. I'll call you at the cabin but please text me when you're there so I know you're safe." Mr. Meyer kisses her forehead and leaves.

Iris locks the door and sits on her bed. She grabs her cell phone and texts Owen:

Change of plans. We're leaving on Friday right after class. Let's get there sooner!

She smiles and turns off her light and goes to sleep.

Owen reads the text and smiles. He'd figure this all out after the weekend. This weekend would be epic and one to remember. Little did he know he was right.

Mr. Meyer heads to his car and sees Dr. Forsythe.

"Dr. Forsythe…. I'm Dawson Meyer's father." Mr. Meyers announces. The men shake hands.

"Yes, Mr. Meyers. I heard Dawson is out of the hospital. I'm glad he's ok." Dr. Forsythe replies.

"I wanted to talk to you about letting Dawson finish the semester," Mr. Meyers begins but Dr. Forsythe holds up his hand to stop him.

"We've been over this before. I've told you and I've told your wife and the president of the university I am in charge of the psychiatric department and I bend the rules for no one." Dr. Forsythe begins to walk away.

"The other teachers had no problem with this," Mr. Meyers tells him and pulls out his checkbook. Dr. Forsythe sees what he's doing and laughs.

"You can't buy me sir," Dr. Forsythe. "I'm not for sale." He walks away and runs right into a man coming the other way.

"I'm so very sorry," Dr. Forsythe says.

"No, pardon me. I apologize," the man says and walks away.

Both men part ways. Mr. Meyer angrily and Dr. Forsythe shook his head, mumbling. The man who ran into Dr. Forsythe goes into his car and watches both men leave. He goes on his phone. "Yeah, it's me. I got it. No…. no problems at all. He doesn't suspect a thing." He listens for a moment and says, "I know what to do." He hangs up and takes out the wallet he lifted from Dr. Forsythe. He is wearing gloves and smiles.

The next day dragged. All Owen could think of was the weekend. Should he tell her right away or by Sunday on the way back? Should he even say anything? Deny till you die, maybe? Finally, the time came and he was out the door. He had already packed a bag that morning so he sat on his bed like a kid on Christmas morning.

"Can I ask you something?" Cliff grinned.

"Yes, she'll be the first," Owen replied. Cliff grinned.

"Do you have protection?" Cliff asks. Owen shakes his head no. Cliff goes over to his drawer and opens it and hands Owen a handful of condoms.

"How much do you do it?" Owen asked, surprised.

Cliff shrugs his shoulders. "Actually…. never." Cliff begins. "I'm still a virgin too but my dad gave me that box as a going away present for college. Both of them laugh.

Owen's cell phone beeps and he reads the message. "Ok, she's here." he sighs.

"Look, the most important thing is to take your time. Let her know she's important and that you care very much for her. Hold her before, during and after." Cliff tells him.

"Got it," Owen responds and heads out the door.

"And remember everything so you can give me pointers," Cliff yells.

"Ok…bye!" Owen yells back, rolling his eyes.

Owen heads out the front door and drops several of the condoms and Iris sees it and laughs. Owen picks them all up as other guys clap. He rolls his eyes and gets into the car.

"Did you want to drive?" Iris asks him.

"No, I'm good. You drive," He smiles at her. They kiss and Iris pulls away from the dorm.

The drive takes them two and a half hours to get there. The weather is colder and snow is everywhere. On their way there, they talk again about their dreams, how they did on finals, and sing out of tune to the radio.

Owen decides not to say anything. They pull up and Iris enters the code on the gate which opens and Owen is in awe of the condos. "What did you say your dad did for a living?" Owen asks, mouth open.

"My dad was a realtor and so was my mom. They're both very good at what they do," Iris tells him.

Owen nods as they go inside. Iris turns up the heat and shows Owen where they'll both be.

"Did you want me to be in a separate room?" he asks quietly.

"No, I want you to be with me," she replies.

"Good, I want that too," Owen tells her.

"We have to get food first," Iris tells him and he smiles.

"Is there a place up here?" Owen asks.

Iris smiles and says, "Get your jacket back on and we'll hit the lodge. They have a small store there and a restaurant. We'll grab everything we need."

They go hand in hand to the lodge. The lodge is huge and beautiful and very busy with skiers and families. They go to the restaurant and read the menu and order and then go to the store and grab food. They head back to the restaurant and pick up their dinner and back to the condo.

On the way out, Owen looks across the room and locks eyes with Aldridge. Aldridge tries to take a picture of them but someone blocks his view. Owen tells Iris that he saw him and she starts to get mad.

"Why are they always …. right there," Iris yells inside the condo. Owen watches her and starts putting the food away. He sets the plates out for their meal and puts the food out. "You can't go anywhere in this town and not run into one of those idiots. Don't they have lives?"

"Your father doesn't know I'm here, does he?" Owen asks.

"No, he doesn't but I don't care. I want you here. I want to be here with you." Iris explains.

They eat their meals and clean up. They have wine and soon they are together in the bedroom. Owen really didn't care about Mr. Meyer or the club or his grades at that moment. All that mattered was that moment with Iris. It was beautiful.

Mr. Meyer wrote down the address on a piece of paper. "Thank you, we'll see you in a bit," and hung up the phone.

"We'll see who?" Mrs. Meyer asked.

"Big property by the lake but it's a way out." Mr. Meyer tells her. She sighed and looked at the clock.

"We were going to the lake today," Mrs. Meyers reminded him. "For the weekend."

"We are. It's only 15 minutes away from their lake house. It's worth $8 million," he whispers.

"Well then…we should check it out." Mrs. Meyers smiled. Out the door they went.

Dr. Forsythe stood at the checkout stand at the Deli on campus. He searched all his pockets. "I don't understand. I know I had my wallet. Where is it?'

"Maybe you left it at home or in your office or car?" The student said.

He sighed and looked at her. "Can this go on my account?" He asks. She smiles and hands him the bag. He gets back to his office and looks around in his drawers and briefcase but finds nothing.

Owen and Iris cooked breakfast and decided to play it safe and stay inside. They closed all the windows and shades and watched TV. They talked, made love over and over again. They laughed and for a moment, the outside world didn't matter.

The doorbell rang and then there was pounding on the door. Startled and scared, they went to the door and looked out the peephole. It was Aldridge. Iris giggled and so did Owen.

"I know you're both in there. Open the door, Iris," Aldridge beat on the door more.

Iris rolled her eyes and then called the Lodge and complained that some drunk was at her door and was scaring her and asked if he could please be removed. Within minutes, security escorted Aldridge away. "You're a dead man, Owen," he could be heard screaming.

"His parents are going to be pissed," Iris laughed.

"Why?" Owen asked.

"His father is a minister and this is going to look really bad. He's going to blow his top on him." Iris laughed. Before they knew it, they were back in the bedroom.

Mr. Meyer looked at the address and just sat back. "Wow, this is beautiful." He explained.

"Breathtaking," Mrs. Meyer added. The gate opened and the two drove in. As the gate closed, the number "22" can be seen on the front in bold metal letters.

The Meyers get out of the car and are met by a middle-aged couple who introduce themselves as Dr. John and Ellen McCallister.

"Dr?" Mr. Meyer asked. "What field?"

"Dentistry," Dr. McCallister replies. "Is that the new Chrysler?" Dr. McCallister walks over to the car intrigued.

Mrs. McCallister watches Mrs. Meyer intently, smiling. Mrs. Meyer grabs her husband's arm. "Why is he wearing gloves?" she asks her husband.

He pushes her away and goes over to Dr. McCallister and says, "Yes, it is. Look at the trim." The men gush over the car as Mrs. Meyer turns to Mrs. McCallister and looks at her hands.

"Why are you …both wearing gloves?" She asks, confused.

Mrs. McCallister puts on a mask and then brings out a baggie and blows dust from it into Mrs. Meyers' face. She suddenly collapses.

"I think something is wrong with your wife," Dr. McCallister says.

Mr. Meyers turns and sees her on the ground and immediately runs to her. "Donna.

Donna! What's wrong?" he screams at her. She has no response. He looks up and says, "Call an ambulance…." and his voice trails off as Dr. McCallister is also wearing a mask. Mrs.

McCallister then blows dust again from the baggie into Mr. Meyers face and he also collapses.

Dr. McCallister removes his mask and gloves and texts:

It is done.

He then puts his gloves back on and they open the back seat and put the couple inside and lean them against each other. Dr. McCallister drives the Meyer's car and Mrs. McCallister drives behind him in a different car.

Dr. Forsythe closes his briefcase and sits down. A student enters the room. "Dr. Forsythe, don't you drive a black Honda CRV?" he asks.

"Yes, I do. Why?" Dr. Forsythe asks.

"Your car alarm is going off," he tells him and leaves.

Dr. Forsythe sighs and heads out the door pulling out his keys. Wrangler watches him and then enters his office. A few moments later, Dr. Forsythe returns and sits down. His foot hits something and he looks down and there is his wallet.

"For goodness's sake," he says out loud. "I'm getting old." He smiles and calls it a night. He grabs his briefcase and opens it. Inside is a gun. Startled, he steps back and then picks it up and holds it. "Where the hell did this come from?" he says out loud.

The door opens again and the janitor walks in. "Oh sorry, Dr. Forsythe, I didn't know you were going to work on a Saturday….. is that a gun?"

"Yes, but it's not mine," Dr. Forsythe replies.

"That's what they all say," the janitor remarks.

"I'm serious, Joe. I've never seen this before." Dr. Forsythe says still perplexed.

"They say that too," Joe remarks. "Maybe you should call the police, sir."

"I think we should, Joe. Would you call them, please?" Dr. Forsythe says. Joe nods and leaves.

Dr. McCallister goes around the corners, heading up to the lodge. He's 2/3 of the way there when he passes a dump truck. He slows down and he makes eye contact with the driver. The driver nods and backs his truck so no one can come up. He then texts someone. Mrs. McCallister honks the car and Dr. McCallister stops and pulls to the side and backs the car up so it appears it's going down the mountain. They hear three car honks and they both get out and move Mr. and Mrs. Meyer into the front seat. They put the car in neutral and push the car over the edge. They both get back into Mrs. McCallister's car and back out and go back down the mountain. They get to the dump truck who now moves out the way.

A line of cars waiting to go up the hill starts as a truck at the top of the mountain moves out of the way to let cars go.

"I love this game," Iris says as she pulls another piece of wood from the Jenga game.

Owen watches as everything falls and gets quiet.

"Owen, are you ok?" Iris asks.

"I have something to tell you," Owen says. "I don't think you're going to like it."

CHAPTER 12
PICK UP IN AISLE 3

Owen raced to the bus stop and the bus had just left. He ran and ran until he got to the next stop. Someone saw him and asked the bus driver to stop which he did. He sat on the bus and thought of everything they had said. He was in deep and he knew it. They were all justifying their behavior to accommodate their sickness. He needed to get out and leave before he was trapped in their world and way of life forever.

He could easily call the police and expose everyone right now at that moment but he knew they could easily find a loophole. Any way out.

Then, he would be in a bigger predicament. He just needed just to get out. He didn't need to be a hero.

He thought of his parents, the University, Cliff, everything. He didn't care about the year he spent at the University. He was ok to move on and just get a job. He thought of Cliff and his parents. He couldn't let anything happen to them. He decided to leave. Just pack and leave. Go to another state and start over. Get a routine job and change his name. Color his hair. Wear different colored contacts. Anything and everything to change and start over.

The bus stopped and he ran over to Iris's dorm. She let him in and hugged him. She told him that she had told Dawson and he actually seemed relieved that their parents were dead.

"I know they put so much pressure on him to succeed. To be a big football player. Be a Doctor. He never got to be or do what he wanted." Iris explained.

Owen said he understood. "What about you?" Owen asked.

"Dawson told me everything. I believe you. I think you just did a stupid jealous thing and just got caught up in your paper and wanted to show your parents you succeeded. I don't like what you did but you weren't the reason for any of this." Iris said, touching Owen's hand.

"I think I am," Owen said, sitting on her bed. He explained everything the sociopath club said about her parents. Owen was sure this was the end but Iris didn't freak out.

"We can't go to the police. You're right; they'll just have each other's back," Iris said, pacing the room. "Then they'll come after you, me, Dawson, your parents. It wouldn't end. They'd still get away with it." she replied.

Owen nodded. "I'm thinking of just leaving tomorrow and break free. Walk away. Start over somewhere else. Change my appearance. Get a new identity."

"Where would you go?" Iris asks him.

"I don't know. Anywhere." Owen tells her. She stops and looks at him. She sits down next to him and holds his hand.

"I'm coming with you. Let's leave tonight. Right now." Iris tells him.

"I can't," Owen tells her. "He's going to text me tomorrow and I'll have to meet him. Then we'll leave. Right after."

"Why?" Iris asks. "If we go now, we can have half a day's head start."

Owen shakes his head. "I have no car. No money."

"I do," Iris explains. "I'll take money out of my account and we'll use my car. Dawson is finishing up this year and then he's taking a year off to find himself. Him and I already discussed that we'll sell the house and split the inheritance. Dawson or the Lawyer will put my share in a trust fund. So, we'll always have money. We'll be set."

"I can't drag you into this any more than I already have. Your parents are dead because of me," Owen begins to cry. "If anything happened to you…."

Iris smiles, "My decision. Ok. We'll wait until tomorrow. But what if they want you to do something like break the law or hide something." "I just won't do it," Owen said.

"What if you're there and you have no choice," Iris asks.

"Ok, let's do this. We'll pack everything and then load the car up. If they text me to come to the club, I'll say I'm on my way and we'll leave. Ok?" Owen asks.

Iris smiles and nods. "Let's go to get all your stuff right now. Then we'll go to my parents and stay there. Tomorrow we'll take my parents' car. They've never seen that one. It's been in the garage for a year. It's their Lexus. The windows are tinted. It's perfect."

"Ok," Owen felt relieved. Within two hours, they were at Iris's parents' house. Owen felt weird being there with her. Iris had sent the workers home for three days so she could be alone.

Iris fixed them both something to eat and within an hour, they were fast asleep.

The next morning, Owens's phone went off. It was a text from Cliff. "Dude, where are you? Are you ok?" Owen texted him back that Iris and him had made up and he would be with her for a few days to help. Cliff responded with, "Thank goodness. I'm happy for you." Owen sent a thank you text back and got up and made breakfast for the both of them. Iris took a shower and got ready. They ate in silence. Finally, Iris shared some of the family photos with him. Dawson and Iris looked distant in all the pictures like they were never happy in their childhood. Owen smiled. He would change that for her. All her pictures with him would be amazing. She would smile in each one. "Just think,"

Iris began. "In a few hours, we'll be leaving this state forever." "Where should we go?" Owen asked her.

"Let's just drive until we find a place we both fall in love with," Iris suggests.

"I like that." Owen smiles. Owen's cell phone goes off with a text.

Meet me for breakfast at Casey's restaurant on 5th Avenue.

A

"It's them," Owen announced.

"What did they write," Iris asks.

"Archie wants me to meet him for breakfast. Someplace called "Casey's on 5th Avenue." Owen tells her.

"I'll map quest it," Iris goes to her cell phone. "Perfect, it's in the middle of the city. Lots of people going to work."

"The restaurant isn't even open yet, is it? It's only 6 a.m. It's still dark outside." Owen tells her.

"I'm looking at their website. It says they open at 7 a.m. and we'll be there at 7 a.m. It's perfect."

Iris tells him. "I'm going in with you," she announces confidently.

"No!" Owen shakes his head. "Absolutely not."

"I'm going in with you. End of conversation." Iris announces and heads to the door with the keys and dangles them.

"I have a feeling I'm never going to win a conversation with you…ever," Owen replies and heads to the door. Iris laughs and they leave.

Owen parked across the street and looked into Casey's. It was a diner on the corner of a low-income part of town. It wasn't far from the bus or train station. Iris looked into the restaurant and counted the people. "I see one waitress, a cook behind the counter, and four customers. One looks homeless and one is reading a paper and drinking coffee possibly, and the other is a couple at the counter ordering food."

Owen looked all around. Lots of cars at the four-way intersection. "This is good. I think we're good. What do you think." Owen asks her.

"I feel good about this. Everyone can see right in the restaurant. Everyone is heading to work. It's perfect." Iris smiled. "You ready?"

Owen looked at her. "They don't know I'm bringing you. They might not like that." "I don't care. You're not going alone." Iris reminds him.

"I think that's Archie at the counter. I don't know that woman who is with him, though." Owen tells Iris.

"Should we just drive away and not go?" Iris asks.

"No," Owen says. I say we go in. It's maybe another member of the club. Maybe someone higher than him. I don't know."

"She's wearing a power suit. She looks like a lawyer or something." Iris says.

Owen nods. "Let's go." They get out of the car and go inside. The bell rings as they enter. Archie turns and sees Iris and stares at Owen who says nothing and heads to a booth directly behind him. Iris sits across from him. Owen smiles at Archie.

Archie turns back around and nods at the Waitress. She goes over to the table and asks what they'd like. Owen starts to get nervous. He looks at Iris who grabs his hand. "We've got this," she whispers. "Order us something like a Danish and coffee."

Owen looks at the Waitress and says, "We'll have two coffees and a Danish."

"Would you like regular or decaf coffee?" she asks.

"I don't care which one," Owen gets angry.

"Calm," Iris whispers.

"I'll bring you decaf. Cream and sugar?" the Waitress asks.

"Whatever," Owen gets more impatient and nervous.

"Cream and sugar would be fine," Iris smiles.

The waitress smiles at her. "On the Danish, we have…" she begins but Owen cuts her off. "I don't give a fuck. Just bring us a fucking Danish. Jesus. You're a Waitress. Can't you just do your damn job?" Owen screams.

The homeless man wakes up and looks over. The man reading the paper looks across. The cook looks down across and says, "You okay, Maxine?"

"I'm fine, Henry," Maxine says and walks away. She nods at the homeless man who reaches up and moves the sign from open to closed. Maxine puts the order on the spindle. She looks at the man reading the paper and hits the counter twice and then her heart twice. He nods. She turns around and stares at Owen.

Iris doesn't see any of this but Owen does. He watches in slow motion as the man who was reading the paper gets up and walks toward them. He reaches into his jacket and Owen looks over at Archie who is now turned in his direction along with the woman. Owen eyeballs her wondering if he had ever seen her before at the club.

By now, the man sits down next to Owen. He is wearing gloves and pulls out a gun with a silencer. Although he is taller than Owen, he moves his body so he's the exact height of Owen and shoots Iris in the chest and in the head. Owen watches as Iris's body falls to the table as if she collapses and falls asleep. Owen knows she's dead.

The man looks directly at Owen and removes the gun clip and hands the gun to Owen. "You son of a bitch," Owen says. "You killed her."

"No, you did," the man says and smiles. Archie and the woman walk up to the table.

Owen grabs the gun without thinking and points it at the man and pulls the trigger. The woman holds open a bag and the man puts the clip into the bag. Archie turns to Maxine and says, "Call it in."

The cook starts closing the shades and the homeless man locks the front door. "You killed her," Owen stammers.

"No," Archie says. "I saw the whole thing. You were fighting with that young lady. You used profanity and then pulled out a gun and shot her twice."

"I saw the whole thing myself," the woman says. "Oh, I don't think we've met. I'm Regina. How do you do? It's such a pleasure to meet you, Owen. I've heard so much about you."

"You fucking sociopath," Owen says, crying and shaking.

The gunman looks at Owen and says, "I'm not a sociopath. I'm a serial killer."

"Oh, Logan how have you been?" Regina asks the gunman.

"I've been Regina. Just got back from California. Laid out in the sun and got a tan," Logan says bluntly.

"You look wonderful, dear," Regina remarks. "Doesn't he look wonderful, Archie?" "He sure does." Archie smiles.

"You people are nuts," Owen cries. He puts the gun on the table and Regina nods to Logan, who is still wearing gloves, picks up the gun and it's placed in another bag.

Maxine is on the phone. "Yes, we need a pickup on Aisle 3. Location is 5th and Grand." Maxine hangs up and nods to the cook.

"Clean-up is on the way, sir," the cook says to Archie.

"Good. Good. Let me tell you what's going to happen now, Owen." Archie begins. Owen stares at Iris and just cries. "Owen, focus."

Logan grabs Owen by the neck. "Boy, you better focus. Instructions are given only once."

"Logan…. temper." Regina smiles. Logan lets go.

Owen looks at Archie. "Here's what's going to happen, Owen. A clean-up crew will pick up Iris. They will take her and dispose of her body. You will go back to school to your dorm room. You will carry on with your life. Your paper is already finished and sitting on your desk. You will turn it in. You will tell your parents you found a job here in the city and will work through the summer as Regina's driver. She pays very well. You will finish your school and become a Doctor. Your parents will be proud. You will forget this ever happened; do you know why?"

Owen nods. "My fingerprints are on that gun and you're going to keep it, aren't you?" Owen says.

"You are smart, Owen. Oh, we're going to get along just fine," Regina replies.

"If you do what you're told," Archie continues. "The gun disappears. The minute you turn on any of us…. on any of the family, the gun and the body reappear. Plus, you'll be held accountable for Barick's murder also."

Owen looks perplexed. Archie sees that. "Your fingerprints on the shot glasses at the meeting house. Your fingerprints on the car, on the gate. I'm sure Dr. Forsythe will play along to get a lighter sentence or a bigger cell with no roommates."

There is a knock on the back door. "Clean-up is here, boss," the cook says.

"Do we have a deal?" Archie asks. Owen nods.

Logan gets up and grabs Owen and guides him around the counter to the back door. "I want to say goodbye to her," Owen cries.

"No, you don't," Logan says.

Archie hugs Regina. "It's always a pleasure, Regina."

"It was so good to see you again, Archie. Take care. Call us again if you need us." she replies. Logan guides Owen out the door.

"It was nice meeting you, Owen. Take care." Archie waves.

"Wait a minute. I'm not going with Archie?" Owen stammers.

"No, dear. You work for me now." Regina responds. Logan puts him in the back of the car. The driver starts the car as Regina also gets in.

Inside Casey's, a group of men in white overalls, wearing gloves, put Iris in a body bag. They close it and take it to the back of a van parked behind the restaurant. A fence is there, preventing anyone from seeing it. The clean-up crew then cleans the entire restaurant lobby and back in a matter of minutes. None of them talk. They all just clean.

One of the cleaners hands Archie, Iris's wallet, rings, watch and car keys. The homeless man walks over to Archie who points to the car. "Take her car and leave it by the airport and walk away with the keys in it." He nods and leaves.

Within minutes, the place is clean and the clean-up team drives away. Archie looks at the cook and Maxine. "You ready?" he asks and they both nod. Archie opens the lock on the front door and puts the sign to open. Maxine opens the shades. Archie walks away.

The van drives by the car Owen is in and he watches as it takes different turns and drives away. Owen looks at Regina. "I'm in for life, aren't I?' Owen asks.

"Sink or swim. Your choice." Regina replies. "Logan darling, where should we drop you off?"

Logan sighs and stretches. "How about the mall? I think I'll go to a movie."

Regina laughs and nods to the driver. The driver makes a turn and they head in the opposite direction where Iris was going. Owen looked at Regina.

"Who are you?" Owen asks.

"My dear," Regina smiles. "Logan already told you. We're serial killers. Welcome to the family."

END

How is a human different from a jackal? Both need to survive in order to live. What if you had to fight for everything you love and desire in order to survive? What if you were put in situations that would lessen your morals and increase the focus for your survival?

People cannot hide their true selves inevitably. At some point, life will test your limits and push your boundaries to see what path one will have to choose, in order to survive. One will not know what they will do until everything is taken away from them to the point where you are forced to decide what's yours and what you will allow to be taken.

Now that you've heard the story of Owens beginning into our family, I want to introduce you to the others. Their humble beginnings and how they came to be, along with my story and my beginning.

I am the Jackal.